The Quilters

WOMEN AND DOMESTIC ART
AN ORAL HISTORY

The Quilters

WOMEN AND DOMESTIC ART
AN ORAL HISTORY

PATRICIA COOPER AND NORMA BRADLEY ALLEN

TEXAS TECH UNIVERSITY PRESS

DL ɥ JB

The paper used in this book meets the minimum requirements of ANSI/NISO Z39.48-1992 (R1997). ∞

Printed in Hong Kong

Library of Congress Cataloging-in-Publication Data
Cooper, Patricia J.
  The quilters : women and domestic art : an oral history / [Patricia Cooper, Norma Buferd].
    p. cm.
    Originally published: 2nd Anchor books ed. New York : Doubleday, 1989, c 1988.
    Includes index.
    ISBN 0-89672-410-7 (alk. paper)
    1. Quilters—Texas—Biography. 2. Quilters—New Mexico—Biography.
I. Allen, Norma Bradley. II. Title.
NK9112.C64 1999
746.46′082′09764—dc21   98-41324
                                                          CIP

    99 00 01 02 03 04 05 06 07 / 9 8 7 6 5 4 3 2 1

Texas Tech University Press
Box 41037
Lubbock, Texas 79409-1037 USA

800-832-4042

ttup@ttu.edu

Http://www.ttup.ttu.edu

For Richard and Richard

PATRICIA COOPER *was a writer and a biologist who taught*
at the University of California at Berkeley until her death in 1987.
NORMA BRADLEY ALLEN *is a freelance writer*
who lives in Cedar Hills, Texas. Both authors were
born and raised in Texas and New Mexico
and have worked actively to preserve the history
and art of quilting.

ACKNOWLEDGMENTS

This book is an acknowledgment of the women and men below. Writing about them, photographing them, talking with them has been one of the most rewarding experiences of our lives.

Interviews: Mrs. Quirl Thompson Havenhill, Mrs. Joe J. (Rosie) Fischer, Mr. Joe J. Fischer, Erma and Leslie Wink, W. H. and Myrtle Thomas, Mrs. A. I. Metcalf, Mrs. Mary Kyle, Bessie Tharp, Mrs. Jewell Howell, Mrs. Harold Neis, Mrs. Myrtle Kelly, Mrs. Hattie Wooddell, Helen Crawford, Delphia Davis, Jo Marie Balfanz, Mrs. T. E. Weir, Mrs. Leona Bailey, Mrs. Iona Chappell, Minnie Russell, Ethel Stone, Mrs. James Webb, Mary Morgan, Mrs. Lois Hand, Mrs. A. B. Cox, Lois Callahan, Mary Peavy, Docia Jones, Mrs. Les Garrett, Stella Fulgham, Mrs. Smith, Eva Drewery, Bertha Carol Kerr, Mrs. Virgil Shurgart, Mrs. Herron, Pauline Moore, Mabel Davis, Mrs. Hattie Winslow, Mrs. Bennett, Betty Lea Royal, Mrs. B. A. Vaught, Thelma Lesley, Lula Crawford, Bea Buferd, Cora Combest, Amy Noll, Mrs. Mary White, Willa Carlson, Sadie Jackman, Mrs. Brenda Wilson, Mr. and Mrs. James Cates, Mrs. Hackler, Mary Woodard Davis, Mrs. Slim (Pearl) Zacek and Slim Zacek, Mr. and Mrs. Arthur C. Woodburn, Rick and Mary Grunbaum, and Marilyn Trent.

Quilting Bees: Mrs. W. M. Garton, Alice Cornell, and Mrs. Vera Leeters taught us a great deal about quilting. For those informative, humorous hours in the quilting house, we thank you.

The Clovis Senior Citizens quilting bee members welcomed us repeatedly, and we would like to acknowledge each of them: Rachel Jones, Flora Gore, Betty Lee, Eula Lucore, Maude Carter, Eva Wilson, Hazel Jones, Eula Judah, Lessie Garrett, Edna Thornton, Edna Paul, Loda Foster, Mary Reed, Bessie Douglas, Thelma Cornelius, Verna Phelps, Cora Blackard, Minnie

Nelson, Ethel Weir, Lou Jones, Winnie Pruet, Cavie Lovett, Jewel Whatley, Eva Brown, Minnie Russell, Tennessee Atkinson.

The Floyd Quilting Bee shared their own quilts and the treasures of their families with us. Our thanks to the membership: Mrs. R. H. Elliott, Mrs. Brooks West, Mrs. Ezra Shirley, Mrs. Slim Zacek, Mrs. Dink Essary, Mrs. H. O. Goff, Mrs. Owen Disney, Mrs. Barto Onstott, Mrs. Tommy Goff, Mrs. Terrell Rector, and Mrs. Onstott.

The Senior Citizens of Los Alamos talked to us at length about the formation of their group, the reasons they quilt, and the methods they use for maximum efficiency of time, materials, and energy. For their warm, responsive sharing in our visits, we thank: Edna Kramer, Marian W. Mullens, Lois Schulte, Olge E. Marlin, Nettie Uher, Dorothy Van Degrift, Mabel Hail, and Laura G. Knolle.

Our friends in Stinnett have quilted together for years. Many of them as children were early settlers in the Texas Panhandle. The following people related a vivid oral history of a settler's life: Bea Turner, Mary Goodwin, Irene Foster, Mildred Anderson, Mr. and Mrs. L. L. Permenter.

Mrs. Arthur Woodburn spent innumerable hours locating source material and organizing for us in advance of our visits. She provided guidance in the history of pioneer settlement in eastern New Mexico. Mrs. Mildred Sparks and Mrs. Odessa Wilman located and introduced us to quilters in their communities.

Caroline Cooper, Nancy Cooper, Marge Parks, Natalie Roberts, and Rella Lossy lent us support and critical advice in editing the tapes. Special thanks to Winifred Bradley Cobb for her work, support, and encouragement.

AUTHORS' NOTE

In the interest of brevity and continuity we have often condensed conversations, monologues, and run-on conversations on similar subjects without indicating that the speaker has changed. We take full responsibility for editing the tapes and our notes in this way. Likewise, we have placed women's portraits in the text in keeping with the mood of the words spoken more often than with the exact words spoken by the woman in the photograph. The portrait of a quilter in every instance may not correspond to the quilt referred to in the text.

CONTENTS

INTRODUCTION

15

CHILDHOOD

27

YOUTH

55

MIDDLE YEARS

87

OLD AGE

123

POSTSCRIPT

155

QUILT INDEX

159

THE QUILTERS

WOMEN AND DOMESTIC ART:
AN ORAL HISTORY

Curry County Museum,
New Mexico, 1974.
Star of Bethlehem quilt.

INTRODUCTION

This book is about a group of women who make quilts in Texas and New Mexico. They are our ancestors. We sought them out because we were interested in their art. We bought quilts from them, sold quilts for them, and in the process became so impressed with their wisdom and strength as individuals that we wanted to record what we could of their lives. Through them we came to know our grandmothers and mothers, and finally to know ourselves. Through long conversations, visits, shared work, we got a sense of our history we had not before experienced.

The book is meant to be a record of the art and lives of women who speak directly to you. We made tapes, took extensive notes, and photographed the women and their environment in an attempt to establish resonances, depths that neither words nor photos have separately. By means of this varied research, we hoped to convey what became the predominant insight for us, that the quilts represent an all-inclusive portrait of these women. The quilts are an artistic expression of their selves and their whole experience.

This book is not meant to be a technical guide to quilting or a history of quilting in America or the Southwest. Since we began our research many excellent books have appeared on the art and history of quilting. Books containing quilting instructions abound. Our interest is in exploring the relationship of quilting to the lives of the quilters.

In the summer of 1972 we met to discuss some plan for work that would bring us together more often, some common task that was an expression of our long friendship. Having just seen the Whitney Museum show of quilts in New York, both of us recognized that the show signaled a renewed interest in quilts, especially in quilts as an art form. We had pieced quilts as children learning to sew, we treasured our family quilts as heirlooms, and had collected numerous other quilts over the years. We began to discuss what each of us remembered about quilting with our mothers and grandmothers. We were interested in collecting new quilts and in preserving old ones, so we decided to start on a venture that would serve those ends, as well as introduce us to quilters, and allow us to participate in bringing these artists the attention they had long deserved.

Norma began immediately to contact quilters and quilting groups in counties around Dallas. She collected quilts throughout the summer, and in the fall we organized a show of Southwest quilts. As we studied the quilts in preparation for the show, they began to take on new significance. Visually they were very exciting. The designs were exuberant, precise, varied. The color combinations as sophisticated, singular, bold, pleasing as any we had encountered. And everywhere the artist shone through, the intent and individuality of her approach within the formal frame of the quilt.

Mrs. Carlson had pieced a Log Cabin from myriad prints to give not only an over-all pattern of straight furrows, but the light-to-dark transition at the furrow's edge was so subtle that from a distance the dark furrows appeared to be mounded. In addition a third over-all design emerged if you looked long enough. How had she envisioned that effect as the quilt lay on her lap in pieces?

Mrs. Wilson was a hard-working woman who lived on a ranch near San Angelo. She pieced and quilted alone, yet she had developed a sense of color and design which made each of her flower gardens a complicated study in emerging and receding forms, a lesson in balancing color tones.

All the quilts as a group looked American to us, but with a regional cast. As we looked longer, we realized that they had certain broad characteristics in common. They were nearly all pieced; very few were appliquéd quilts. That is, pieces were sewn together to make a regular, repeated geometric pattern as opposed to pieces of fabric cut into shapes and sewn on to a common fabric ground. The pieces themselves were squares, rectangles, triangles joined together in the block style. Such quilts can be made either by forming a single pattern in a block and later sewing these blocks together to form the whole, or by joining pieces together progressively as in Baby Blocks or Trip Around the World. Either form exhibits the most efficient method of joining together straight-edge forms: a savings in time as block quilts are faster and easier to work than fancier appliquéd quilts, a savings in space as blocks are quite portable for working in the lap and can be stacked neatly in minimum space until time to put the quilt together, and finally a thrifty use of fabrics as even the smallest piece can be cut to fit in on some straight edge.

The average age of the women who had made these quilts was seventy-three years old. Most of the women making fine, traditional quilts were themselves pioneer-settlers of the land, or had come as children with their parents to homestead in the last quarter of the nineteenth century. The quilters still worked out of piece bags containing scraps their mothers and grandmothers had placed there. The quilts were a compendium of family history, each person symbolized by a bit of textile.

In addition to thinking about the quilts as a record of family and community history, and as a repository of American design and textiles, we began to understand the quilts as art coming directly out of the home, out of familial interactions. The quilt was made for a member of the immediate family, for a close friend, or a dreamed-of mate. In this context the home was studio, art school, and gallery. We knew from our own experience that the technique of stitchery was passed on by exacting instruction; so also was education in color and design. And the art was controlled and handed down by women, usually mother, grandmother, or aunt. The best elements of teaching were often combined over the construction of a quilt: early and often loving instruction, tradition, discipline, planning, and completing a task, moral reinforcement. Quilting was a virtue. The pioneer home must have been a particularly challenging place for inventive design under the pressure of necessity and scarce materials. As we continued to study the quilts, then, we became more and more interested in talking to quilters about the experience of creating quilts.

Other questions kept coming to mind. Were the women aware that they were professionals? Artists? Did they know [that] they were stitching together the history of the country, making the great American tapestry? It became vital for us to talk with these women. We wanted them to tell us all about it; we wanted to get a close look at their lives.

In the spring of 1973 we drove out from Dallas toward the Panhandle on the first of four trips to photograph and talk to the quilters. We made contacts through our parents, through quilters Norma had met on the first trip to the region, through the local newspapers, and by just asking around in a small town. We talked to approximately thirty women at length, sometimes spending several days in a home if we were invited. We visited or participated in four quilting bees. All the women we talked with were articulate, informative, responsive to our questions and interest. It was no surprise to them that we were interested in their work. They were used to community recognition in some cases, and in others a lonely quilter might simply state that she knew the work was good, that she was pleased at the sudden renewal of interest nationally in quilts, but for her the pleasure was in the doing and that was where she took her satisfaction. Lois Callahan made a typical comment:

"Well, it wasn't too surprising that folks would get interested in quilts once they got interested in history again. My kids always showed an interest in the quilts, if they hadn't before, once they was interested in family history."

As the quilters talked about quilts they were constantly reminded of some other parts of their lives, a story about pioneering times, an anecdote about a family member, or some technical detail of quilting. The quilts seemed to be the format in which they had condensed much of personal, family, and community history. Talking about the quilts often triggered memories of stories they had heard from their mother or grandmother over the quilting frame. That common task which had brought them together to sew also brought them together to talk and exchange stories. In a similar setting they passed on to us what they had heard.

We never knew when we were going to gain new understanding about the quilts. In the fall of 1974 we attended a quilting bee in West Texas. Early in the morning we arrived at the house of a woman whose quilts were exceptionally impressive. She pieced designs of unusual originality. We had been told her husband was also a quilter. The house was small, crowded with evidence of many projects in progress . . . wood carving, small-appliance repair. A quilting frame occupied half the living room and the other half contained two recliners facing a television set.

Sitting at the Formica table in the kitchen drinking coffee, we began to examine her collection of quilt blocks. Each small hand-sewn square contained a different design. The squares were stacked one on top of another in labeled boxes for easy reference, an index or catalogue of quilt patterns. She was interested in attempting most new patterns that came her way, as well as inventing designs herself. Long ago she realized she would never complete a quilt of each pattern, so she had settled on making samples of many patterns. She let them sit around for a while and finally decided which one she would piece and put in the frame for quilting. Her husband was badly crippled from arthritis but could "still push a needle right smart." He had been a farmer until his retirement. We looked at the quilting both had done and were unable to distinguish between their stitches.

He explained carefully that he didn't take part in the design, choice of pattern, or color composition of the quilts. He just helped by carefully sewing along the chalk marks his wife had drafted. Later as I started out the door he took my arm and explained again, "I only do the quilting. She's the artist. She's the one that makes the light shine."

We found generally that members of the family were very supportive of quilters. Mr. Cates, a cowboy, explained to us, "I'm glad Molly got to show you that quilt, but I won't let her sell it. That's the finest thing we ever had in this house. That's the best one she ever done. We had that one on our bed from the first till I told her to put it away for safekeeping. The gold triangles was beginning to show a little wear. No, we'll always keep that one."

We stayed with Mrs. White for two days in her small frame farmhouse. Late one night we spent some hours looking at each of forty-five quilts she had made for members of her family, her legacy to them. Each quilt had a handwritten card attached with a note to the person for whom the quilt was intended. Some of the notes were poems. All were messages of love. We lit the kerosene lamp and sat down around the kitchen table to drink coffee and continue to talk.

Mary explained that quilting was an expression of how she saw the world. "You can't always change things. Sometimes you don't have no control over the way things go. Hail ruins the crops, or fire burns you out. And then you're just given so much to work with in a life and you have to do the best you can with what you got. That's what piecing is. The materials is passed on to you or is all you can afford to buy . . . that's just what's given to you. Your fate. But the way you put them together is your business. You can put them in any order you like. Piecing is orderly. First you cut the pieces, then you arrange your pieces just like you want them. I build up the blocks and then put all the blocks together and arrange them, then I strip and post to hold them together . . . and finally I bind them all around and you got the whole thing made up. Finished."

Late in the summer of 1974 we were on the high plains of Texas, looking for a little farm where Mrs. Wilman quilted and kept chickens. We had been told she had quilts from three generations out there and that she still quilted daily herself. The house was a small, wooden, three-room, white painted structure set right down in the dirt with a few shrubs around. As far as you could see in any direction was flat plowed land. The house had been there a long time by local standards, probably built right on the site of the dugout of the original homestead. Mrs. Wilman peered through the screened door at us. We explained that Mrs. Hammond had sent us, and that we were looking at quilts and talking with people about them. The strained suspicion disappeared from her face and she unlatched the door to the screened porch which stretched the length of the house front.

We stayed three days. She could make the rooms come alive with her talk. As she related her life and the history of her family, all the themes, fragments, fleeting insights merged into a whole for us. We saw the pioneer woman and the artist.

"I'm making grape jam. You'll have to talk while I work. I was the oldest child of a family that had settled in West Texas in 1890. My folks came from Springfield, Missouri. They wanted more land, their own land. My daddy used to say, 'I don't know anything more satisfying than your own land as far as the eye can see.' They were after acres of their own. In the Southwest then, if you were willing to work hard, you could make a fortune. My mama was newly married and came from a big, white house in Springfield with elm trees in the front yard and lilacs all around. She was for moving west to where they could get ahead and get something for the kids. She was lively and had been a tomboy in her family. I don't think she was afraid of anything, but she always said nobody could imagine then what you was getting into out on the plains of Texas. She hadn't even talked to anyone about what it was like in this area before they set out. She told about starting out in the covered wagon with one bedstead and a lamp given to them by her mother, and all the quilts she had made for her hope chest. They had two wooden trunks full of tools, seed, and utensils for the house; Dad had his plow knocked down inside the wagon and his hoes, shovels, and ax strapped to the side. On the back they tied a cow, and a team of mules pulled the wagon.

"Mama had her piece bag with her on the whole trip and was working on this Star of Bethlehem I have here. Later I come to call it the Lone Star when I made it. She was still working like she used to at home with little tiny fine pieces out of that quilt bag. By the time she got to the edges of the star she was piecing pieces to get it finished. From then on, until neighbors moved nearby in 1910, she was piecing from our worn-out clothes and work clothes with a little bit of fabric thrown in from when Dad got to town and could afford some yardage.

"She used to talk a lot about that first year. Seems it stood out in her memory so clear, and that was the year I was born.

"She used to tell how when they come finally to the homestead and the wagon stopped she felt so lonely. There was emptiness as far as the eye could see. How could a human endure? There wasn't even anything to hide behind. The color was dull yellow and brown. The sky was always changing. Out here you notice the colors always changing because there is nothing else to look at but the things you make right around you and the sky. You can see the weather coming . . . dust storms, northers, rain, tornadoes, and twisters. In those days you could see anything that stood up against the horizon. The fence rows and windmills stood out for miles, and in that time you knew where folks had settled by the windmills. The houses was built underground and called dugouts. Or they would build a half dugout, finishing the top part with lumber and sod and tar paper.

"My papa worked on the well and building the windmill first. They had to have water. He had help from the Thompsons who rode two days to get to our place. Mama said one of the great pleasures of her life was putting her face in that first bucket of water.

"The first summer Mama worked with shovel and pick to build the dugout. Papa was out there to start a ranch, and he went right off looking for cattle to make a small herd. He began to put in feed crops right after they put down stakes. He would dig when he could but Mama worked at it every day. That and the garden. She was putting in seed too. She says most evenings she barely had strength to get her clothes off before she fell asleep. They could hardly bear to eat or fix food they were so tired.

"Mama used to say, 'Don't stop now or you'll never get going.' When we had a long, hard job coming up she would say, 'Mary, we won't sit down today.' Sometimes when the work would get too hard, I would ask 'Why?' And she would say real quiet, 'Because you just have to. There's nothing for it but to do it.'

"When the dugout was just big enough to stand up in and braced with wood, she put in the bedstead and the quilts and had a good day's rest. Papa made a shelf for the lamp. There it sits over there on my table now.

"Mama said she thanked the Lord that the first dust storm didn't come up till late that summer. She would have turned right around and gone home if she'd seen one first off. It was just like now, you know, only worse because the farms, sodbusters, hadn't planted much yet, and the sand was mixed with plowed dirt. Oh Lord. At the horizon the dust came up like a yellow band between earth and sky and then it kept on rising and rolling toward you till you were right inside it. Small and large twisters and tumbleweeds all mixed up with it and the sand sifted into every pore in your body. I always know one is coming because the light changes. It gets yellow and real still all around. When the sand hits, it's dark and cold. She hated being underground but she said at least you didn't hear the wind so loud. The sand would sift in through the door until you felt buried alive. No wonder they got out of those dugouts so fast. Folks never lived in one any longer than it took to get some time, lumber, and tar paper together.

"The first time Mama was left alone was when Papa hitched up the wagon to go after firewood. Up in the breaks there was wood and you could haul back enough for the winter in one trip. It was a week in all there and back. That was late September. Mama had her garden in and she was plowing more land for corn when the first dust storm came up. The wind blew for three days so hard and the air was so full of dust that she had to tie a rope around her waist to get out to feed and milk the cow. There was nothing else but to endure it. She had never heard sounds like was in the wind. She took to quilting all day every day. She used to say, 'If I hadn't had the piecing, I don't know what I would have done.' There was nobody to talk to and no where to go to get away from the wind except underground. She got to worrying about freezing to death in the winter. She used to laugh when she told it, how you never saw anyone quilt so fast in your life.

"Mama's best quilts were her dugout quilts because that was when she really needed something pretty. She made a Butterfly and a Dresden Plate and a Flower Basket during those two years in the dugout. After a while she got to like the sound of the wind, if it didn't go on too long, and she could get real soothed with that sound and the needlework at night sitting by the lamp. She made the Basket for Papa. She started the Butterfly in that first dust storm all alone. She couldn't see how the garden was gonna survive the wind and she knew the trees she had planted were done for. One lived though; that pecan right out there. I water it every day. The Butterfly was free and fragile. It was the prettiest thing she could think of. She knew I was coming along and the Butterfly was for me.

"She didn't want a baby to be born in the dugout, but I was. And it was one more winter before they got aboveground. She said she just wasn't gonna live underground with a baby, but they couldn't get crop or cattle money and the lumber was expensive. That second winter was hard. They planned the house and she quilted everything she could get her hands on, just for warmth. This house was made just like she planned it."

We looked around us and realized she had laid the groundwork for the house with her quilts. If she had not quilted and planned quilts through those bad times, maybe she would have been planning how to get out of that country. The quilts were her base and from them she planned and completed her next project, the house. At each step she sank her roots deeper into the earth.

At each level she changed, built her surroundings. She structured her surroundings. Oh yes, then the community came next. Roots reaching out from one ranch to the next, from one house to the next . . . a whole network, a grid of support. A quilt. In our imagination we rose over the house and looked down on the patches of land spread flat out like a good quilt as far as the eye could see.

Patricia Cooper/Norma Buferd

Berkeley, California
June, 1975

CHILDHOOD

Mrs. James Webb,
Clovis, New Mexico, 1975.

When I was little we had dark comforts made from old overalls and wool trousers on our beds. Sometimes the neighbor women would come in and quilt with Mama. Now them quilts was always real pretty. I wanted to keep some of the pretty, bright-colored quilts but Mama would say that we could make do with what we had. Others needed them more.

My mama quilted every day until I was four and the third child was born. Then there was nowhere to put the frame up and leave it. One day a week, when the neighbors came to quilt, my brother would take the bed in Mama's room down to the kitchen and put up the frame for that day. It was quite a job, but he never minded. There was no more than four women working because there was no room for more.

I remember standing in the doorway with my thumb in my mouth watching them. Sometimes I waited and waited for the women to go home because I was hungry. But it wasn't proper for a child to ask for food when there was company in the house. Dad was always proud of Mama on quilting days. When he came inside from work he would say how busy she had been. He knew that she had a hard and lonely life; he was happy that she could enjoy quilting. When neighbor women came over for the day, he was glad she could have a day with her friends and enjoy herself. He always spoke kindly to ever' one.

They took all the pretty quilts to the Baptist Church. They was for the poor people and foreign missions. And sometimes if somebody lost their house to a fire or a twister, the women would all go with a stack of quilts and say, "These is a gift from the ladies of the First Baptist Church."

*Tumbling Diamonds,
Texas, c. 1910, Cooper and
Buferd Collection.*

*Quirl Thompson Havenhill
quilting Eight-Pointed Star,
Clovis, New Mexico, 1973.*

Texaco Church, New Mexico, 1973.

Stars and Hexagons,
New Mexico, 1975.

I was supposed to write a story one time about when I was born. I went home and asked Daddy. He said I was born in a half dugout about ten miles north of where this town sits now in the middle of winter. That winter was so cold that all Daddy's cows froze to death and he skinned them and put the hides on top of the dugout to make it warmer. I wasn't about to tell them about that kind of stuff to let 'em laugh at me. So I said that I lived in a big house with pillars in front and rolling green lawns that went down a big hill all the way to the road.

Last year my husband went all the way to Europe on a cattlemen's convention. He wanted me to go but I'm too Scotch, and anyway, they was all going on a tour and you had to do just what they told you every minute. I stayed home and quilted all the time . . . made the most beautiful quilt, a Colonial Lady that could have lived in that white house with the pillars.

Farmhouse in the high plains, Texas Panhandle, 1974.

They just don't know what I'm gonna do next. The funny thing about livin' in that dugout was now I can appreciate it. I didn't ever get that feelin' that Mama said she had about being closed in down there under the ground. To me, being just a little thing, it seemed the safest place in the world. I don't know how I come to be ashamed of it by school age except that we had been living in town for a while by then and I got the idea the town houses was supposed to be better, higher class, you know. But one thing you was safe from was the tornadoes in those old dugouts, and many a wind got rode out down there.

Come to think of it, I don't remember any trouble or distress from those early times. Although I know the grownups felt it. There was so many stories about rough times when they first settled. All I can see from way back then is the light playing on the low ceiling and Mama's back bent over her sewing next to the lamp. I slept with my sister and she must have loved me 'cause I can remember on the coldest mornin's, she would get out of bed and warm my clothes next to the fire. When they were good and warm, she would stuff them under the quilts next to me so I could dress up warm before getting out of bed.

Well, you didn't have much space, but you had your family all around you.

I'll tell you what held your life in this country, honey. A windmill . . . no life without it. I remember so clear, and I was just a little tyke when we moved to West Texas, out near Runnin' Water Draw. That was a funny name for it because Runnin' Water Draw never had no water in it, except once in a great while when we had a rain. Then it flooded all over the place.

My daddy decided to dig his well right down in the middle of the Draw. He figured that the water wouldn't be so far to reach. Up on the high ground he couldn't have dug it by hisself. The water was there, but what he

Birds in Flight, Texas, 1965,
made by Irene Foster.

Texas Panhandle, 1975.

didn't figure on was that the sand down there was kindly like quicksand and kept seepin' back in the well. Even now I don't know if I'm more scared of quicksand or scorpions.

When the wind blew the water was pumped into an old wooden barrel down on the ground. That barrel was always coated with green mossy stuff. I'll never forget the way it smelled . . . and what my face looked like in the water.

From the time I was about ten years old my job was to hang a bucket on the spout and climb the tower when there wasn't no wind. I had to turn the wheel by hand. I've seen a growed man slung thirty feet to the ground if the wind happened to come up while he was on top. Me, I'd just grab aholt and ride the thing round and round till the wind would let me off.

Sometimes the worst happened and the well would bust. Then the whole family would take the milk cans, put 'em in the wagon, and go borrowin' from the neighbors. Nobody ever asked to be paid back though.

Crazy Windmill, Texas, 1945,
Cooper and Buferd Collection.

I can remember even back before I was old enough to quilt, my mother and older sisters would be quiltin' and us little ones had to keep their needles threaded. We'd be out in the yard playin' and they'd holler they needed some needles. We had a whole bunch of needles that we'd run in and thread and stick 'em on top of the quilt for them. Then when they run out of needles threaded, here they'd holler again.

There was six girls and one boy in my family. We all quilted and pieced together. I can remember Mama even saved her strings and cut them into long, thin strips for some pattern she had in mind like a Log Cabin or Windmill Blades. Then she would cut me a square piece of paper and I'd sew them strings across there in rows. They had to be the same width that I'd measure with my school ruler. I can remember it just as well.

My husband tells about the time he got sick with the measles. He was six years old. His mother set him to piecing a quilt and every other block he set in red polka-dot pattern. Said it was his measles quilt. He wouldn't like me to tell it now I know. But lots of cold nights when I'm at the quiltin' frame on one side of the fire, he pulls his big old chair up on the other side and cuts pieces for me. He's even done a bit of piecin' from time to time.

It's a sight, that big old long-legged man with his boot toes turned in to make a lap to do his piecework on.

We've got a fair long road from the highway and three loud dogs out there. They all always sound off when somebody turns up our road. And let me tell you, he can git rid of that work quicker than a gnat can bat an eye, when them dogs commence to barkin'.

Plumb tickles me.

Windmill Blades, 1875, donated to Cooper and Buferd Collection by Docia Jones, New Mexico.

I like straight-line quilts. The first quilt I ever worked on was like that. Papa was setting up fence around the place he homesteaded, and Mama decided to

Log Cabin, straight furrow, c. 1900.

Field near Fort Sumner, New Mexico, 1973.

make this fence-row quilt. That's when I started piecing, when I was five years old. And it was a piece of work we all did together. I asked her in later years what she did with those stitches. She said she just left them in the quilt, 'cause she liked to see them reminding her of that time. She never took out any of my stitches, though maybe she had to quilt a little closer to make it look right.

I really settled into quilting when I was fifteen at my school. Our teacher was very interested in that kind of thing. Needlework she called it, and we each made one handmade quilt that year. We had to piece and quilt the whole thing by ourselves, and she was real particular about color and stitching. You had to take them stitches out if they wasn't straight and true and even. Come to think of it, she was the one that first told me piecing was like art. She valued it like drawing. Looking back I guess that was kind of an advanced idea. But then it just seemed natural.

We girls thought she was fine. If we couldn't find just the right color, she'd let us look in her piece bag. Seemed like her materials was always the best. It meant a little bit of Miss Jessie in your quilt.

The boys gave her a hard time. Some of the boys in those days was big strappin' fellers before they got to the sixth grade. And it took some doin' to keep 'em in hand. She managed by threatening to send 'em home. If you got sent home, you had your daddy or your mama to deal with.

My mother died when I was four and my stepmother had other kids, so I just had to learn to piece by myself. Right after my mother died my father lost everything he had . . . except eleven dollars, thirteen head of horses, and five children. So he left and went to Indian Territory. He sent for us when I was six. I rode there in an ox wagon. My grandmother drove 'em. We'd driven for three days when my grandmother said, "I think I see your father coming this way horseback." And it was and he pulled me from that wagon and gave

Mrs. Lois Hand,
Plainview, Texas, 1975.

Ninepatch, New Mexico, c. 1875,
Cooper and Buferd Collection.

me lots of hugs and kisses. I hadn't seen him in more than a year. I won't ever forget my sixth birthday.

I remember my mama, even though I was only four when she died. When we moved from Bosque County, when I was ten, we went through great towns of nothin' but teepees. Just Indians, they would just be squatted around there and cookin' on that fire, smokin' on their pipes. Just havin' a good time, I guess. I was kinda scared. They looked different, you know.

We had two wagons, and another family with us had one. We got within fifteen miles of where my dad had bought a place and a big storm struck us there. We stayed all night in the yard of a family that lived there. They had a big family there in a dugout. One great big room under the ground. We eat with them and it snowed so much we couldn't get out for days. Dad finally got out on horseback and found our place and took us there. And when we got there we thought we had a haven of rest. And we did. We had a log house. It was one step down in the ground. We lived there a year. Then he built a house of real lumber.

Back in the old days we had to make the quilts so thick. You know in those old dugouts the wind would come through so bad that you really had to be covered to sleep. Papa would bring the cotton back from the gin, you know. Just how ever much Mama needed. It was all clean then. You know nowadays some of the cotton you buy is knotty. It's bollie. That's where they pulled it boll and all. We used to pick it out of the bolls and it would be nice and smooth. Now they have machines to do all that . . . and it's just not as good.

We stayed busy every minute we had quilting. We all worked in the fields and mother didn't have any idle time. If anything let up, she was working on her quilts.

Oh, and after being in the field all day we'd be tired, so tired. And cold.

Cotton bolls at Halfway Co-op Gin in Halfway, Texas, 1974.

In the morning we'd get up and go to the field. Papa would build a little fire and it'd be so cold you'd just freeze standing there. Hands so cold you couldn't pick. We did all wear long-handled underwear and thick cotton stockings that came up high under our dresses. We wore long dresses then, all the way down to our ankles. Course, we weren't allowed to wear pants. But I've thought about it a lot of times. I don't know if I would venture out now, if I had to go into a cotton patch again. Course as short as they wear

Cotton trailers at Halfway Co-op Gin,
Halfway, Texas, 1974.

their dresses now, if you bent over you just as well put on a pair of pants. Yes, pants would have been warmer. . . . We just weren't allowed.

It sure did get cold when the wind was up.

When I was about four years old the neighbor's baby died, and all the women was called in to help. Mama knew what her part was because right away she took some blue silk out of her hope chest. I remember that silk so well because it was special and I got to carry it. When we got to the neighbors some of the women was cooking and the men was making the casket. Mama and three other women set up the frame and quilted all day. First they quilted the lining for the casket, and then they made a tiny little quilt out of the blue silk to cover the baby.

Windmill on high plains
in the Texas Panhandle, 1973.

Crazy Quilt, Texas, c. 1910,
collection of Mary and Rick Grunbaum,
The Great American Cover-Up, Dallas, Texas.
Photo by Jim Reynolds.

Windmill near fence made of cable spools, Stinnett, Texas, 1973.

I don't use a compass to plan out my circles. Sometimes I draw around a plate if it's the right size. Sometimes I take my drawing board, put a tack in the middle, tie my string to the tack, and circle at the end of the string. That way I can make 'em as big or small as need be. Then I plan whatever pieces I'm gonna do inside the circle.

One time I made a Dresden Plate that like to never circled. I had them center edges about a sixteenth of an inch off. I watched my papa build a wooden windmill when I was little, and he had the same problem. Oh, how beautiful that windmill was when he got it finished, standing up against the sky. It meant water, you know. But it really just looked pretty by itself . . . tall and with the top turning this way and that, whirring around.

Back then I slept in the attic room. There was windows at each end and I had my bed under one of them. I could hear the windmill at night. That sound was my lullaby. The windmill seemed like the biggest circle then, bigger than the moon or a wagon wheel, and always in motion.

Windmill on New Mexico cattle ranch, Santa Rosa, New Mexico, 1974.

I'm eighty-three and I've done a heap of quilts, girl. But I remember, like it was yesterday, my first quilt. Mama had one of them frames that swung down from over the bed and there was always a quilt in it. She quilted for the public, to help pay our way. Now, we might take one out late one night when it was finished and wait till mornin' to put the next one in. But that was as long as it ever was.

Mama was a beautiful quilter. She done the best work in the county. Everybody knew it. She never let nobody else touch her quilts; and sometimes when she was through quiltin' for the day on a job that she liked a lot herself, she would pin a cloth over the top of the quilt so nobody could look at it till she was done.

I always longed to work with her and I can tell you how plain I recall the day she said, "Sarah, you come quilt with me now if you want to."

I was too short to sit in a chair and reach it, so I got my needle and thread and stood beside her. I put that needle through and pulled it back up again, then down, and my stitches were about three inches long. Papa come in about that time, he stepped back and said, "Florence, that child is flat ruinin' your quilt."

Mama said, "She's doin' no kind of a thing. She's quiltin' her first quilt."

He said, "Well, you're jest goin' to have to rip it all out tonight."

Mama smiled at me and said, "Them stitches is going to be in that quilt when it wears out."

All the time they was talkin' my stitches was gettin' shorter.

That was my first quilt. I have it still to look at sometimes.

Molly and girls, c. 1920, family album photograph, Patricia Cooper.

Sunburst, New Mexico, c. 1930, made by Pearl Zacek.

YOUTH

My daddy was a Baptist preacher. I reckon you can tell that by how ornery I am. We didn't have much luxury, I can say. But I remember the funniest day one time when I was still a young girl.

Mama was goin' to help me start my quilts for my hope chest. She had got the old scrap bag out. We spread 'em all out on the bed and tried to kinda put the colors together right. But the scrap bag was really low. We sure hadn't got anything new in a long time and it seemed at that time every-

57

body in the church was usin' all their own scraps and none had come our way.

Mama said, "Come on into town with me Saturday, and we'll just pick up a few pieces of brighter calico to spruce 'em up a bit."

Well, come Saturday, true to her word, we went to town with Papa. Soon as he tied up the team he went over to the feed store and we went to the dry goods. We had picked three pieces of remnant blue and was just fingerin' some red calico. We was jest plannin' on enough for the middle squares from that.

Just then Papa come in behind us and I guess he saw us lookin'. He just walked right past us like he wasn't with us, right up to the clerk and said, "How much cloth is on that bolt?"

The clerk said, "Twenty yards."

Papa never looked around. He just said, "I'll take it all!"

He picked up that whole bolt of red calico and carried it to the wagon. Mama and me just laughed to beat the band. Twenty yards of red. Can you imagine?

A Baptist preacher, jest like any other man, likes that red. We had red for a long, long time.

My mother didn't have any quilts to give me when I got married. There were still small children at home. Of course, I was just a child myself. She gave my younger sisters each a quilt made from their baby dresses when they left home. My mother-in-law gave us enough quilts to go on our bed to keep warm. She had a big family too, eight children, but she had a man to help. She was from slavery days, which I guess caused her to use every scrap of every kind . . . blue jeans, wool trousers, things like that.

I had my husband saw me some frames right away. I had been saving

Hattie Wooddell
on her front porch, Jacksonville,
Texas, 1973.

my special scraps for a long time and I made us a Double Wedding Ring. It was real pretty and he really liked it too. Then the first baby was on the way and I made a Dutch Doll for her.

Since then I've always had a quilting frame up somewhere in the house. Even when I was the milk inspector for the whole county I found some time each day to work on my quilts. Working on them made some pretty bad times seem better to me. If my fingers hold up, I hope to make the best one yet.

Hattie Wooddell holding her Double Wedding Ring, Jacksonville, Texas, 1973.

Tree of Life, Stinnett, Texas, 1975, made by Irene Foster.

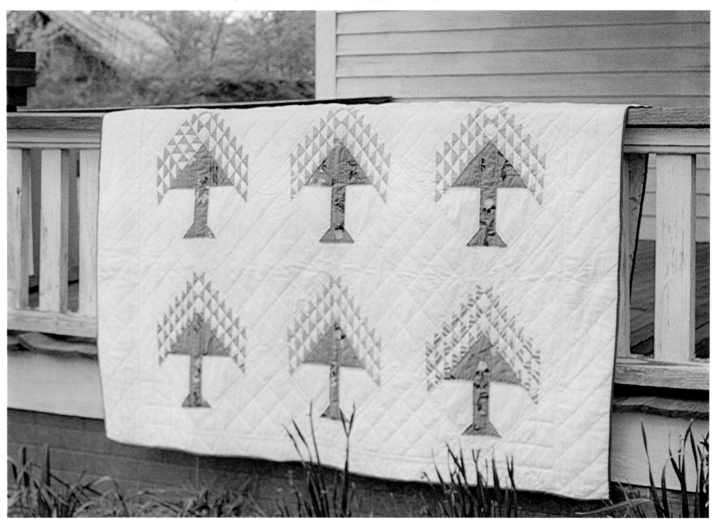

Wellman Texas School, c. 1900.

Odessa at school, c. 1900.

Mother wanted to teach me how to quilt, but I didn't want to learn. I had dreams of teaching and making a big salary. I didn't ever want to be dependent on a man. Mother smiled and shrugged, but didn't insist. From about eight years old and up I worked in the fields, pulled cotton, and cooked all the evening meals. My sister did the house cleaning mostly. During the depression, Mama couldn't quilt any more. There was no hired help to be had because they wouldn't let blacks spend the night in town, so everyone in the

Schoolhouse, Oklahoma, c. 1930,
Brenda Kerley Collection.

62

family worked in the fields. In those days people often paid their debts with quilts.

The young girls would make Friendship quilts for their hope chests. They would all get together in the Community House or the church to quilt them together. The boys were allowed to pick them up and walk them home. . . . "Seeing Nellie Home from Aunt Dinah's Quilting Party."

I do recall that in March, that first year I taught at Hunter School and lived in the teacherage with Miss Stewart; we almost froze to death under twenty quilts. We could hardly turn under them. It was thirteen below zero and the snow was blowing through the cracks and the wind was blowing out the kerosene lamp.

The schoolhouse wasn't much better. The school board had promised me when I went there that the facilities were adequate for thirty-five students. Well, that first year we had over forty students; the number was always changing with the crops and the weather conditions. Some of the poor little things came without enough clothes to keep a flea warm and we couldn't seem to keep the wind out. We'd just have to pull up our chairs around the stove until I got fed up. You know, people were interested in having their children educated but times were so hard and everyone was struggling so to get settled in the town that seems they just didn't have that extra effort. The school board was men, and I went right around them to the women at church. Before Christmas that first year we organized an auction at the church. Folks brought canned goods and fresh baked goods and quilts and whatever they had to auction off for the school.

We worked up a quilt for that auction. All the ladies made up a block and we pieced it at the church Wednesday nights.

What we bought with the money was tar paper to cover the cracks and another potbelly stove for the back corner of the room. In the spring we added a room on the side and everybody helped. Oh, I remember we had so much fun on that one. I was courting my husband then.

Mrs. Smith
with her Ocean Wave,
Jacksonville, Texas, 1973.

Before my father died, he was a lumberman; we lived in a forest near Lufkin. He built our house. It was a log house and it was plenty big, two fireplaces. He had plans all laid out to make it bigger when the family grew and when he could get the time.

He put such care in fittin' everything just perfect. He always whistled when he worked. Sometimes he and Mama would whistle harmony. We all turned to listen to that when it happened. I was always allowed to choose if I wanted to work outside with Papa or inside with Mama. When I was younger I dearly loved workin' outside with him.

65

Log Cabin,
light and dark variation,
New Mexico, 1973,
made by Mrs. L. L. Permenter,
collection of Willa Baker.

*Log cabin made of
hand-adzed logs, Montana.*

Well, every time I make a Log Cabin I think of him. It just comes naturally, making a Log Cabin. When my mother became a widow woman, she quilted very little. She had seven children, and I guess you could say we were poor then. We had to have quilts 'cause that's just what we had to keep warm. Sometimes the neighbors would come in and quilt and help her get ahead with the bedding. They wouldn't let me quilt without lessons, but there just wasn't time for my mother to teach me how. I just stood there with my nose over the frame.

I don't remember any courtship quilts. The young girls weren't even interested. They didn't quilt anything fancy, just what was necessary. That was all they had time for.

The way my first quilt come about had to do with growing. Before we was old enough to sew, Mama taught us to garden. She had nine kids and the field hands to feed, so she put in a big truck garden every year. All us kids had to work in that garden beginning around age eight; but before then, when we were just small, we each had a little flower garden to tend. Mama loved flowers, but she didn't have time to work them herself, so she put us little kids to learning gardening on flowers.

Well, we quilted in the winter mostly. And when it came time for me to piece my first quilt, it was a Flower Garden. My fingers just wanted to work flowers. All the pieces in my first quilt was flowered prints.

When it was cotton-pulling time, Mama and us girls would go out in the fields too. At that time we was just pulling cotton enough to fill the quilts. Now that turned out to be a good lesson learned because later in the depression, after I was married, I pulled cotton for money, and I didn't mind it so much as them that had no experience.

Anyway, Mama showed us how to pick the best cotton for the quilt

68

Log Cabin quilt
on oldest house in Curry County
New Mexico, 1974.

West Texas cotton farm, 1974.

batting. Then at home we cleaned and carded the cotton, working it till it felt like a soft cloud. We could all help with that. Even the men used to like smoothing and pressing the cotton with their hands. When the pieces were carded into about one foot by five inches, we laid these side by side and slightly overlapping on the quilt backing until it was completely covered up. Then we put the pieced top on like a sandwich, and rolled the whole thing up until the quilting bee.

Back when I was a girl quilts was something that a family had to have. It takes a whole lot of cover to keep warm in one of them old open houses on the plains.

When a girl was thinkin' on marryin', and we all done a lot of that, she had to start thinkin' on gettin' her quilts pieced. The way I done mine was real nice, I think. Papa had laid up a beautiful arbor with the brush he had cleared from the land. It was set up a ways back of the house. Well, I jest went out under that arbor, set up my frame, and went to quiltin' outdoors. Now some thought that was real funny, but I sure thought it was nice.

Mama gave me one real beautiful quilt, a Lone Star that she had done herself. I made three by myself that I don't reckon were much to look at, but I was awful proud of them then. And that's what I set out with when I married my sweetheart. Now that's a story. You won't believe it to look at me now, but I married me the finest-looking young man for three counties around when I was eighteen. And I didn't meet him at no dance neither. I don't reckon I would have stood a chance there. These big size tens were never so graceful. They're just good strong platforms for standin' on.

Anyways, what I was doin' was settin' there under that quiltin' arbor one spring afternoon, April fourteenth, just quiltin' and dreamin' a dream on ever stitch and just plannin' who might share 'em with me.

And this deep, fine voice says, "Pardon me, ma'am, but I've been seein' you out here ever day for weeks and I jest got up my nerve to come over and speak to you and see what you were workin' on with such care."

Lordy, girl, I married him and, as I recall it now, that was the longest speech he ever said at one time to this day.

Lone Star, Texas, 1970,
made by Bea Turner.

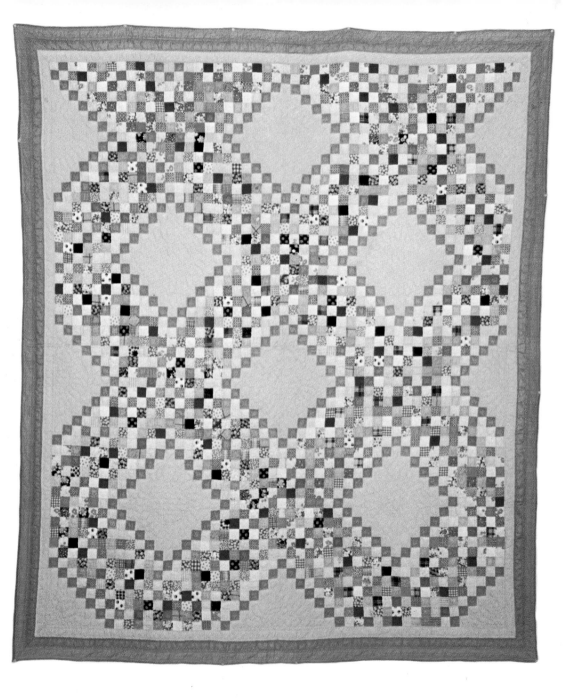

We were living out in the country when we first married, and we just didn't have much. When the kids started coming along there was lots of quilting to be done.

For a while I pieced on the halves for people around. Some folks were doing better than us, and they would get together enough material for two quilts. I would piece both of them, and for my work I got to keep one for nothing. Then one time Mama came to see me. I told her what I was doing. She said, "You're not going to have to do that any more!" Later, after she went back home, she sent me out a great big flour sack stuffed full of scraps. It was a gift that always meant a lot to me.

Now I have some ten big scrap bags. If someone else were to see them, they would seem like a pile of junk, but I've got all my pieces sorted according to the color. Got my cottons here and my polyester's there. I've been told I have a way with matching up my colors. It comes natural to me. I keep figuring and working with my materials, and thinking about my colors a long time before it feels right. I know how my quilt is going to look before I ever start.

Different ones of my family are always appearing from one of these bags. Just when you thought you'd forgotten someone, well, like right here . . . I remember that patch. That was a dress that my grandmother wore to church. I sat beside her singing hymns, and that dress was so pretty to me then. I can just remember her in that dress now.

My mama pieced this one, set it together, and I quilted it. I wouldn't take nothing for it. It was the second quilt I made. In the summers we'd put up the frame on the screened porch, and when the work was done, Mama would say, "O.K., girls, let's go to it." That was the signal for good times and laughin'. We'd pull up our chairs around the frame and anyone that dropped in would do the same, even if they couldn't stitch straight. Course we'd take out their stitches later if they was really bad. But it was for talking and visiting that we put in quilts in the summer. People would get out after the chores in the summertime and how the word would fly that we had the frame up. Had to have a screened porch 'cause sometimes you'd quilt and visit till midnight by lamplight with the bugs battin' against the screen.

Before I married, Mama taught me how to embroider and crochet too. This is a round-table cover and this is a library-table runner. I took this out of a magazine. My magazine was late getting to me that month. My mother worked in the post office and she had copied this piece of lace right out of it before I ever saw the pattern. Then I made it. Her and me and one other lady is the only ones ever been able to make that pattern that I know of.

Well, anyway, I was dreaming on havin' all kinds of pretty things in my home after I married. Well, I found out right quick that livin' out on a farm, what with all the chores that had to be done, a person didn't have a whole lot of time for makin' pretty things.

But let me tell you, I got it all worked out with a little thinking. I had to drive one of them big wheat trucks during harvest. I would just take my piecin' or crochet to the truck with me in the morning. Then that way when I had to wait for the men to load or unload the truck, I would just be piecin' on my quilt top. They would all look into that truck and laugh. I'd laugh with 'em. That way I got my quilts done.

Rosie Fischer,
Rowlett, Texas, 1974.

Happy Union cotton gin, Happy Union, Texas, 1974.

Star, Texas, 1974, made by Rosie Fischer
and photographed in a cotton wagon on the Fischer farm.

Mrs. James Webb,
Clovis, New Mexico,
displaying her
Trip Around the World, 1975.

I'm jest settin' here piecin' some more of these tops. I always seem to do this same one. It's called Trip Around the World. It's easy done for crippled fingers and somehow it jest seems right for me.

I was born on a mountain in Arkansas. I don't hardly remember being a girl. I was married to a man when I was not quite fifteen year old. I was figurin' a while back and I reckon he was thirty-two at the time. I suppose I liked him some then; I don't know. But I was jest like all the rest of the girls on the mountain. We thought if we could get married and leave home we wouldn't have to work so blasted hard. Ha! Little did we know what kind of work we was gettin' into. I had the first baby nine months and eighteen days after we married, then another one in a year; and then I believe it was two that died. Three more years and another boy.

We all did field work. I love field work. I wish ever day that I could do it still. Choppin' cotton, and pickin' it. I really like to pick cotton, but I'm too old for field work now. We used to take the babies to the field with us. When they was little, I would always try to find the coolest, shadiest spot around, put a quilt on the ground, leave 'em some crackers, when we had some. And they would play there all day. Each one soon as he got big enough would come on to work with us. I patched 'em up some cotton sacks that wouldn't drag too heavy on 'em when they was first startin'.

When the depression come we heard we could do better in Oklahoma, so we rode on a truck with some folks up there. But, oh my, it wasn't no better at all. The mister got some of that work around, finally. They called it the WPA, WPO, something like that. Jest workin' on the county roads or cleanin' up a small patch for somebody. Jest country work.

I got so mad at that man sometimes I could have jest beat him up like a man. But I never did. I don't guess I ever raised my voice.

I've lived now in Arkansas, Oklahoma, Texas, and New Mexico, and I think one of my boys has a girl that lives in Chicago.

My daddy filed on a quarter out in New Mexico when I was little. That was around 1895. We lived in a half dugout then. And my, my, the wind would just blow, and the tumbleweeds grow, and people were always losing their hats. It was the kids' place to chase the hats. And we'd just run and laugh, hoop and holler. Oh, we had lots of fun back then, we kids did, just growing up, you know.

There was ten in our family. I was the oldest. We picked cotton, hoed cotton. Honey, as far as I can count back, I never went to school more than twenty-six months in my life until I married.

My husband and I had three children when he went to school to learn to teach. When he got out of school, I said it was my turn. He commenced to teach right away in a little one-room school that was out in the country a ways. We had quite a bit of fun then. I'd go into his school sometimes, and he would have all the children down on the floor. I can just look back and see that group yet sitting on the floor and laughing up at me.

Well, once I finished, we taught school together until I was sixty and then they made you quit. By then my husband was a Nazarene minister besides teaching school and running the farm. The last twelve years of his life, he was in a wheel chair and I took care of him. We did a lot of quiltin' together then. It was so much company for us to be together. I wonder if all that hard work didn't just cause him to break down. He stayed with it all day and then he'd study for his sermons at night.

We raised a fine family and had a lot of fun in that little school. When he was crippled they wanted to put him in a rest home and I said no. No rest home. I'll crawl before I'll give him up.

Trip Around the World,
New Mexico, c. 1935,
collection of Winifred B. Cobb.
Photo by Jim Reynolds.

Mrs. A. I. Metcalf, Clovis,
New Mexico, 1974.

Texas Panhandle, 1973.

MIDDLE YEARS

*Detail from Album quilt (left) owned by Jo Marie Balfanz, Clovis, New Mexico.
This quilt was made in 1970 as an exact replica of a quilt
made for her father in 1900.*

Two or three months after we homesteaded here in '90, Mrs. Wilcox told me about Pastor Williams. He was a big person in our lives—the traveling Methodist preacher. Well, a finer man you never saw. He had a head of hair into his eighties. I recall when we had my sister's wedding he was supposed to join 'em, when a late norther came up, blowing sleet and the wind piercin'. Well, he come through. Traveling those long distances from one part of the territory to another, and always helping out when he could. If you had a wagon stuck in the ditch, he'd pitch in same as any man after services or before for that matter. He always just come and went . . . on to the next congregation that needed the word.

Well, Mrs. Wilcox got the idea to put up a quilt for him. Something special. We only had time to quilt for cover in those days settlin' in. They weren't pretty. But in this quilt we did for the pastor we outdid ourselves appliquéing each one of us a block. And we sent out the word by him along the circuit for ladies of other congregations to send a design for the top; he could carry them little appliquéd pieces easy in saddlebags, no weight to 'em. We gathered it all in and put that quilt together. That was a feat in those days. He said he never seen anything so pretty. It was a treasure.

Later when we got our church built, we put together lots of Album or Friendship quilts for folks getting married or moving away, but they never took the place of that first one.

There wasn't no choice about finishing this house. Mr. Thompson and I, we worked side by side all them years. Up till I was sixty-five. He taught me everything I know about building and carpentry. We was more than married; we was partners. When he died, we was in the middle of building this house for ourselves, and after the funeral I come home and put on my overalls and finished this house in thirty days. I never looked up till I was through. I lost fifty-seven pounds during that time. Then I took up quilting.

I plan my quilts just like I used to plan a house. Folks say, "How come you quilt so good?" I say, "If you make careful plans, it will come out right."

Everything has a time. I get all my work done in its proper time. I get up at five in the morning and head for the back. Early in the morning I like to be with my flowers and grapevines. I do the trimming and weeding, mowing and cultivating. When all my chores are tended, it puts me in mind to get to my quilting.

Quirl Thompson Havenhill,
Clovis, New Mexico, 1973.

*Fanfare, New Mexico,
1973, made and designed
by Quirl Thompson Havenhill.*

*Home of Mr. & Mrs. Joe J. Fischer,
Rowlett, Texas, 1974.*

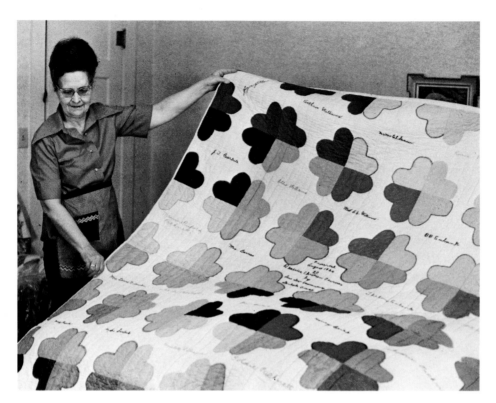

Bea Turner holding Friendship quilt made for her by friends.
Stinnett, Texas, 1973.

I hardly have a room big enough to put up a quilt frame in my house. That's why my husband finally built me that quilting house out back. When we first come here, I just had my frame hanging from the ceiling over the bed, so I could pull it down over the bed and quilt. My husband never could understand it, but I just quilt for myself. Sometimes if I have a color scheme

Sunbonnet Sue, Texas, c. 1930.
Photo by Jim Reynolds.

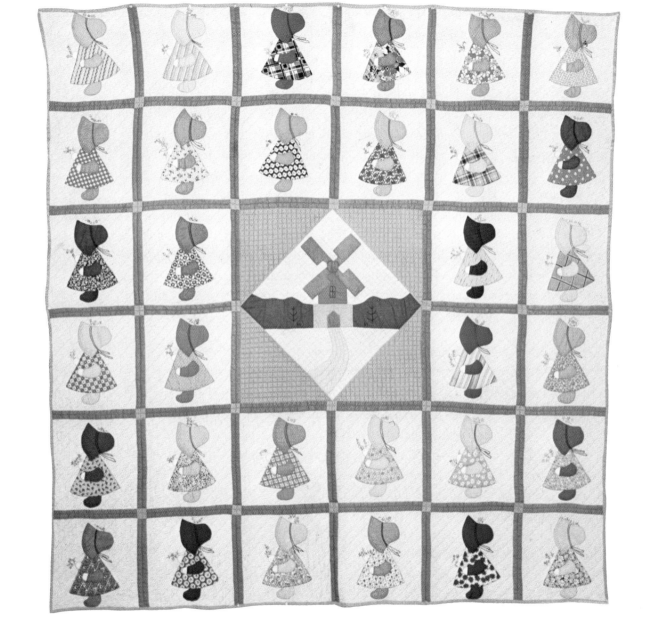

working I can get my house work done and be ready to go to piecing by 7 A.M. I always like to get my colors worked out. Now and then he gives me a hand.

I've lived in three towns in my life and I've got three Friendship quilts that each place gave me when I moved. My name's in the middle and even the men signed and sewed their own blocks. Not many of them living now.

I'm making a big quilt for my other grandson with big red stars in the four corners and a goose chase all around. A friend of mine who draws real good is makin' me a buffalo to go in the center because that's the name of his football team.

For my little girl grandbabies, I'm making quilts for their dolls and buggies. I make about six at a time with little girl things on 'em. I tell you, they're just darlin'. I do the little Sunbonnet Girl pattern a lot, and ever one of them is a little different. I make some little change in the pattern. The hat or the foot turned a certain way will give each little girl a personality all her own.

Gabe and I got along fine. He used to call me Baby. He'd come in the kitchen and say, "Baby, get off your feet." Then he'd make me and him a glass of iced tea. I'd sit down at the table or take up my piecin' in the rocker. He was always in favor of my quiltin'. I was strong and able and could have worked all the time in the house or fields, but I needed to take time out for my quilts. They give me so much pleasure and relaxation. Gabe and I would help each other and then we'd take a little extra time for ourselves. Lordy, how we worked them early years. We always found it easy to talk. I was grateful he never took advantage of me.

Now my sister's husband was different. Always complaining and never there when the kids died or she was sick. He would bring home guests by the wagonload and expect her to cook for them on the spur of the moment. Well, that's another story and I feel sorry about it. When he died, she found there was no money, so she took in boarders. She made her house into a boardinghouse. At that time in this town there wasn't nothing else to do except teach school.

After Gabe died, I went out and lived with my oldest boy and his wife. They was really strugglin' out there on that dry land trying to make that cotton grow. They needed help in the field. And I sure didn't mind doing it.

Late in the day at pickin' time my daughter-in-law and me would pick out some of the best cotton and take it to the house. Then when supper was over, we'd sit and card it out real smooth. There was just wire things on them cards, like a comb has on it you know. It taken a good long time to do it, but it looked so nice when you was done.

Lordy, I remember one time we'd finally gotten together a whole roll of cotton and stored it up in the attic till we could get through with the cannin'. We went up there to get it and the rats had made a nest in it.

Well, we'd of like to cried, but both of us just sat down and laughed and laughed. Then we started cleanin' it up.

We got some fine quilts out of it too. Course we always had fine quilts in our family, if I can brag some. My mama brought fine quilts with her when she come from Nebraska in 1891. She was a wonderful cook. She spoiled Papa for anyone else. He just lived alone after she died. Said a man could be satisfied with one good woman in his lifetime.

Well, about the quilts. Mama had the smallest stitches and the smallest feet in the country. She was particular about everything she done. I got that from her. There was an order to everything, and when one of her quilts was done, it was just like the rest, all of a piece and finished right—the corners turned to a tee, like making the bed, ever seam straight as an arrow; you know it wasn't hard to stitch good and it was real satisfying to keep everything up to standards.

Straight-Furrow Stripe, Colorado, c. 1870, collection of the Pioneer Museum,
Colorado Springs, Colorado. Photo by Bill Helms.

Cotton field on Texas high plains, 1974.

Now back here in the back room I got all my materials stored. I put every scrap of material I think I can ever use into them piece bags till I can get to sortin' it. Then I put it into those boxes. Kinda on file. I got my boxes fixed up neat in case anything happened to me. Someone could tell where everything was and what they could make use of. Each box is labeled with the colors of pieces inside, and then some is labeled with plaids and stripes and the kind of pattern if they's already cut. I like to keep my pieces up. Don't do to have lots of little worthless pieces lying around. So when I get to the bottom of the bag, I make a string quilt. Oh I've made all different kinds of string quilts. You just pick up all the leftover pieces that's too small to cut a pattern from and you put them together however looks pleasing. This quilt right here now, I thought to set them strings together to make a bigger pattern and it turned out real pretty. You can use up your strings when you're just piecing for cover.

Now these are for my sunlight and shadows in the Log Cabin. I'm gettin' close to the bottom on my lights. I've got plenty of darks. I have to keep my eyes open for lights. I always know what shade will match what I got in mind. I never buy for my piece bag and I hate to borrow. I like to think I can take care of myself.

It's so much fun to pick up these quilts and see everybody's dresses in it. Oh, here's one of mine when I was sixteen. Mother saved pieces from every dress she ever made for me; when I got older she gave them to me to make a quilt. In her day pieced tops were all made from a woman's scrap bag, and at that time, more often than not, the linings were other old worn-out quilts or old blankets. We never wasted a bit of cloth . . . used it over and over until it wore out. Waste not, want not.

That sayin's old as the hills and I got it from my mother. She sure taught me how to save and she knew it from hard experience. I come here as a baby with my family. My mother had been livin' in this white frame house in

Strip Circle, Texas, c. 1910.
Photo by Jim Reynolds.

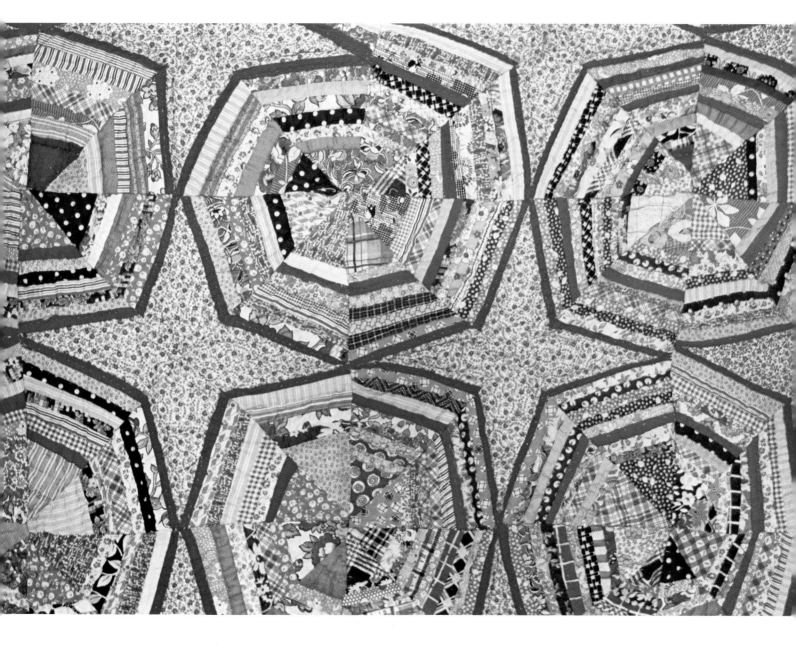

Josephine, and she moved from there with her whole family, from East Texas to New Mexico, in a covered wagon in 1905. There was me and Mama and Papa and Uncle Wes with his wife and baby (that was Nancy Caroline), and then Uncle Ben and Grandma.

They spent that first winter in the dugout. My aunt came out in the spring and she says they were all on the edge of despair when she got there. Wes's wife and Mama both had gone dry and couldn't nurse the babies. Auntie had brought the cow and we all got fat. Auntie put everyone to bed by turns in the big bedstead they had brought with them; that was the only furniture in the dugout. She nursed 'em back to health.

The second winter the women and children stayed in the dugout again and the men had scraped enough lumber together to build a lean-to for themselves against the cattle shed. They spent the winter up top tending to the stock. That was a better winter.

But they put up the house that spring. They moved in then. I can remember that time. Little things seem important. Like when my papa lifted me up on the horse with him and I could see all around. All our land stretched out flat to the edge of the sky.

I belonged to this club out in Hamilton. It was just a quiltin' club. Everybody taken a covered dish and we just quilted. Whoever had the club put up a quilt, and we quilted it out. Sometime we'd quilt two a day. Some days they would be fifteen or twenty of us all over that quilt. Some of 'em didn't do too good a quiltin'. When it come my time I didn't put up no fancy quilt. I just put up one I didn't care how was quilted. Lot of 'em did the same thing. I'd put up a string quilt, or just something I didn't care who quilted on it.

I remember a girl. She was newly married. She had a baby and she joined our club. She had never quilted before and I don't reckon she'd ever seen anybody quilt. She'd belonged to our club, I don't know how long, two or three weeks or maybe a month, before she found out we was going down from the top and plump through the lining with each stitch. You know what? She was workin' on all her stitches so hard and they was just goin' through the top . . . jest quiltin' along on the top. Would you ever think there could be anybody that dumb? She was a sweet little ole girl, but she jest didn't know no better. "Well, I didn't know you was goin' all the way through," she said. Why everybody in that room jest died. I laughed and everybody did. It was funny, but I felt sorry for her, she hated it so bad.

I've always belonged to some quiltin' club or church bee. When I was raising my kids the club was always my time to get off and get some relief. I ain't happy doin' nothin'. But if I can take my relaxation with a needle and have some fun talkin', then I think it's all right. This club here now hasn't been going too long but we're gettin' to know each other. Sometimes I sneak off and drive out to Hamilton to visit the girls there, catch up on all the news, and quilt a bit. We got this project here now to finish up by Christmas for the orphanage and then we gonna get to work on quilts for our spring auction. The ladies at the First Methodist are havin' a big barbecue-and-bake sale for their new Sunday school wing, but we always raise more with our quilts for the building wing. Oh, I shouldn't be talking this way.

I'm goin' tonight over to Ella Daniels' house where we're having a community get-together for her. She's going over to Corsicana to teach school. It'll mostly be young folks there but I'm her Sunday school teacher so they invited me too. I'll be takin' her these cross-stitched dish towels. Done 'em in her favorite wild flowers. She'll get a kick out of that. The young girls still appreciate needlework, although they don't gather in clubs much the way we used to. I could say they run around too much if I didn't like to run around so much myself.

No, sir, I'm not tired and I do enjoy gettin' around. Today I'm going

Iona Bailey and Bea Turner, Stinnett, Texas, 1973.

out to the historical site at the fairgrounds where we're restoring that old-timey house for the fair. Give the little kids some history to look at. Lookey out there in the shed behind the mattress and you'll see the old sewing machine I'm takin' out. One of the first Singer models ever made. And notice that milk can. Got that from the Johnson's. Her papa had it on the wagon when they come out here, leading the cow behind. Did you visit our old dugout on Highway 2? We did that last year. Here take this book about it. Really it's just a pamphlet, but it's got all our memories in it about that time. We're gonna sell it at the fair. It's a bargain at a dollar.

My Sunday school class did a quilt for the teacher for her Christmas gift. But a lot of girls came that never had quilted. Held a needle, maybe. And law, some of the stitches that went in that quilt you wouldn't believe. But it was the thought that counted, and the fellowship. She was really thrilled when she opened the box.

We used to quilt up there at the Methodist church. You know, making quilts to sell to get money for the church. I just went up there and helped them some. Everybody would take a dish and I really enjoyed it. Lots of talkin' goin' on. We just talked about everything.

When I was growing up I used to walk four or five miles down a cow trail to church. We didn't care. It was a lot of fun. Course, I don't guess we went to church more than about once a month. That walk was a time for the sisters to get off and feel free. We would talk about everything.

We used to supply a lot of houses with quilts from the church.

One time we quilted for a widow lady that was under hard circumstances, too many kids and no man. Or if someone new came to the community and was setting up housekeeping, the women of the community would do a Friendship quilt for them. Each woman would make a pieced block of a design they had agreed on and would embroider her name in the center of it, and often the date too. Then we would all quilt it together and give it as a community-church gift.

During the depression and really hard time, people often paid their debts with quilts, and sometimes their tithe to the church too.

Well, we got together not long ago to embroider a quilt. Some of the girls that didn't know how to embroider got the dinner on the table and kept us in Cokes and coffee, stuff like that to help us along. We got the most of it done the first day; there was twenty of us working. And the second day we worked in the morning. All but four of us had to leave at noon, so us four decided to eat out rather than at the church. Well, we went down to the

Church, Megargel, Texas, 1975.

Nettie Uher, Los Alamos, New Mexico, 1975. Photo by Bill Helms.

Burger King and that's where you punch a button to give your order and then punch another button and this little train goes. I think you're supposed to put your money in the little train. We never did figure it out because we punched the wrong button the first time and I tell you we laughed till we were weak. We never did eat. One girl laid down in the back seat and said she didn't want to be seen with us. Just things like that is so much fun.

Later that day we finished the quilting and took it out of the frame and set down in the middle of the floor to begin hemming. Someone mentioned that silly train again. I thought we'd never get that hem done for laughing.

You know this quilt we did for our Bible teacher? It was just out of love and appreciation for her. She taught us the Bible once a week and we didn't pay, or nothing. She taught because she was so full of it and she just couldn't get enough of talking about it. Anybody that wanted to come could come. She just loved to teach the Bible so well.

Gettin' together like that, unless you done it, you don't know how much fun it is.

After my boy Razzie died when he was fourteen, I began to quilt in earnest, all day sometimes. There was still the two younger ones to take care of but losing my oldest just took away something. I lost my spirit for housework for a long time, but quiltin' was a comfort. Seems my mind just couldn't quit planning patterns and colors, and the piecing, the sewing with the needle comforted me. That's when I learned I'd rather be makin' things than growin' things. Although I still garden and enjoy it. I put in my sunflowers and zinnias every year. But not a truck garden like I used to.

Dr. Cooper was practicing medicine in Josephine then and being the wife and nurse for a country doctor, I'd never had time nor need to quilt. We was often paid in quilts for services, and when I got more than we needed, I'd pass them out again. One time a big tornado struck the county

107

Sunflowers ready for harvest, Texas Panhandle, 1975.

Rebel Patch, Texas, c. 1865, owned by Mary Goodwin.

and some of those little towns was leveled. Lord, it was a sad mess. I went along with Doc to nurse. I had stacks of quilts in the wagon ready right then for the emergency, and I was cutting up them quilts for bandages before the day was over. Some was used for bedrolls. Folks couldn't do any better than just to roll up and sleep right there on the ground so they could start rebuilding. The only thing worse than tornadoes is drought.

I keep my best quilts put up for special occasions, or just to bring out and look at, put on the bed once in a while. I'll pass them on to the kids of course. They each have an heirloom picked out. But in those busy days before Doc passed away, I had lots more everyday quilts made of outing and feed sacks and wool suitings. We used them for pallets for the kids to crawl around on. And we wouldn't think of a picnic without a pallet. We used to

Sunflower, Texas, c. 1940,
made by Erma Wink and photographed
on the ranch of Leslie and Erma Wink,
Robert Lee, Texas.

take a pretty quilt out to the mesquite thicket for a special picnic when we was courtin' and put an old quilt under it. Lord, was that pretty on a spring day.

Mabel, someone's got to be responsible for checking all these pieces of red.

Do you mind if I go ahead and cut this in the middle?

No just take these scissors and cut there, and then do it like this. Now how many needles have you got threaded there? We want to work right along and just be able to pick 'em up. Oh, someone has dropped a stitch here. Some say it's bad luck.

Now don't reach too far over the frame there to tack; it's too hard on you.

We've made two hundred and thirty-six quilts for the orphanages since 1971. We often get one done in a week. We started out with just two coming up here and now we've got a group of fourteen most meetings.

All the materials are given to us. We get materials from lots of people in town. The Catholic church here has been very generous. They save and give us a lot, and one little lady brings them over to us every now and then. They bring a big sackful. We have everything in there you could ever imagine or couldn't imagine. And I sort mostly. I have so much fun. I hold up the garments if they are whole and try to get someone to put 'em on. Of course they won't. But if they're well made, we don't cut them, we just put them in the Goodwill 'cause they can use them whole.

We sort what's ours into heavy and light cottons, corduroys, outing flannel, and whatnot. Then we have lightweight blankets or electric blankets

Marian W. Mullens,
Los Alamos, New Mexico, 1975.
Photo by Bill Helms.

Los Alamos Senior Citizens quilting bee,
New Mexico, 1975. Photo by Bill Helms.

Tillie Gonzales, Los Alamos, New Mexico, 1975. Photo by Bill Helms.

that we pull the electric parts out of for the inner lining. Things are so high now we can't buy the batting. One lady does the linings and sometimes she has to patch and piece to get a big enough lining. We do pretty well.

Now sometimes we have long strips left over because we use mostly big blocks and we have some little pieces left over. So what we do is sack them and then I call Mary, she's such a darling; we can't bear to throw anything away, so I says "Mary, you just have to help me." So she takes the sacks down to Santa Fe to the Goodwill. They make rugs (braided) of the long narrow strips and they also give pieces away for quilts . . . and then the littlest pieces they grind up and sell to a roofing company. That way we use up everything.

Give her some coffee so's she'll stop talking.

You know, quiltin' is scarce these days. One of the little boys that came to play with my grandchildren saw me quiltin' the other day. He said, "Are you makin' a blanket?" He'd never seen quiltin'. The other day my little grandgirl was here and she was occupyin' herself drawing while I quilted. She brought me the drawing and said, "Mamaw, here's what you look like." She had drawn me quiltin' even to my bare feet under the frame.

Some of the ladies is into crocheting beads. I can't see any use for that.

I'm taking my quilt along on the hunting trip. Sonny's gonna get married one of these days and I'm not gonna be ready. I'm doing him an Album quilt. Ever piece is different.

My first mother-in-law painted a quilt with crayons. She drew it on cloth and ironed it to make it fast. She set it together with green and I got it quilted for her. It's the most unusual quilt I ever seen.

Iva Smith, Los Alamos,
New Mexico, 1975.
Photo by Bill Helms.

Rosie Fischer
holding the Quilt Trip,
Rowlett, Texas, 1974.

Come and get this food while it's hot.

They had a family reunion out at the Milton Place for Granny Milton's eighty-fifth birthday. All the kids come, and she had thirty-two grandchildren and forty-six great-grandchildren there. They said the church was full of her kin.

I do my blanket stitch around the Butterfly. My son's got a Pansy quilt that he just loves. Did the blanket stitch around that too.

She is just a darlin'. She does everything sweet. He don't treat her right but there's no use talking about it. Some people was born mean.

Now wouldn't this make a beautiful quilt. If you just placed dark triangles next to these diamonds, they would stand out. They all need proper blocking. This calico would do for the border. Better use these old fabrics before they rot. Oh, didn't she take even stitches.

Cotton is what you want for sure. You can't hardly buy good cotton no more. I take it right from the field and card it to get the very best. I can't find it good enough in the stores any more, and I certainly don't need to go north to buy cotton. I like it long and silky, and it should press down smooth and flat.

I do remember now that we used to pick out feed sacks and flour sacks. They were made of good strong cotton, good enough for everyday quilts. We sewed sacks together to back quilts with when we didn't have any other backing, and we would pick out different brands of flour depending on how good the sacks was.

During the depression, of course, the feed sacks were made of printed

118

Cotton at the gin
in the Texas Panhandle, 1974.

Diamond Field, New Mexico,
c. 1955, made by
Quirl Thompson Havenhill,
Cooper and Buferd Collection.

cottons, and many's the time I've gone over a load of feed down at the store trying to match up a quilt color to one of them prints.

I quilt with a thimble with cotton stuffin' in it to keep from making a wart on my finger. With a good strong quiltin' needle, I can whip through a quilt in no time, especially if it's my own. One time I quilted a whole quilt in one day . . . all day and all night. I just lined up chairs all around the quilt and just moved from one chair to the other and didn't even have to break my thread.

When the cotton's sufferin', we all feel bad. We sure need that rain. It just seems like it comes as far as the Red River and stops. One time I saw a drought so bad all the trees died.

Now this here will go in the frame as soon as that one there goes out. This lady wants me to do one by Christmas. And then I want to do the little granddaughters some special quilts out of velvet. Here, look at this one. I've almost got it done and I've got three more just like it cut out. It's a new one for me, this velvet. I never done one like this. I'm always excited to get at somethin' different. I never like to do two of the same ones. Now here's the Double Wedding Ring I'm piecing. I think this is the prettiest thing I ever did if I do say so. If I can just get to them, I'll be happy.

If I'm not busy, I'm wanting to be. But I'm never rushed, honey, because I'm constantly thinking. Thinking doesn't require your hands.

Today I made cream cake and coconut cake and angel food cake. I make cakes when ladies order them from me. I've got five pecan trees outside and ever year I make pecan pies. But you know, the very best pecans come from New Mexico, not Texas. You can freeze pecans and that's how I put 'em by.

These here tea towels I embroidered when I was small. You know you could always ask my daddy for money for needlework. If he knew that I was learning something, he'd find money for the materials. He always had money for embroidery thread. What I embroidered I got to put in my hope chest and keep. I learned to embroider in Bible school at the First Baptist Church in Oklahoma. Mama would give me the flour sacks to bleach and make into tea towels.

Now I started quilting with Mama before I even started school. She'd put my piecework in her quilts too. We used fabrics from feed sacks mostly. Mama saved pieces from every dress she made for me and my sister. And then when we got older, we all pieced a quilt together.

I planted me a garden this year and I'm hoping for some rain.

My friend from the Methodist church come over this morning to help me hoe. She said we're goin' to have a community quiltin' soon at the church. Guess I'll take a dish and go 'cause I really enjoy it. I went out in the country with my brother-in-law and his wife not long ago and saw two girls I used to run with before I was married. We just knowed each other all our lives, so we visited there out in the country. When I got back to Houston, my brother-in-law said, "What'd you all talk about?" I said, "Don't ask me what we talked about. We talked about everything under the sun. I don't know what we didn't talk about."

I enjoy being with my friends more than anything. We can talk about anything with each other. I can remember we used to walk through the creek bottom talking. You know how I got my quilts when I got married? We lived out in the country when my sister was sick and they didn't give showers like they do now. You just had your own hope chest and you had to fill it. I had four quilts when I got married. I quilted three and Mother gave me one. That was enough to start house with. I had to supply all my kids when they got married, and when my sister's house burned, I set her up again with quilts.

When we was down in Austin, I noticed this house across the street from my granddaughter. It was an open house, open day and night in this here development. You could see plumb through it. But it wasn't to welcome anybody; it was just for show. Folks must miss real open houses.

OLD AGE

Willa Baker running on a country road.

Lord knows, honey, I never quilted when I was a child. Not me. I was the one ran outside and stayed gone most of the day until I was old enough to work. Then I took up working in the fields alongside the men. I was always the big woman and I couldn't be cooped up in no house. Why I never picked up a needle except to mend until I was sixty-five and took to quilting. Now I can't stop.

Everything I ever learned about building and plowing goes into these quilts. Except colors; them colors is all mine. Now I like to try to put them colors down in a way no one ever saw before.

Sometimes I quilt for other folks. They say, "Miz, you got to do this one for me. Can't no one quilt like you." And I do it for them, but even before I start I'm thinking about getting back to my own work. I do all my own quilting and piecing, you know. I know it ain't neighborly, but I can't let no one else touch it.

That man there can't hear nothin'. We got the money together one time to get him a hearin' aid. He wore it for about a week and then just set it

Mary Kyle, Texico, New Mexico, 1974.

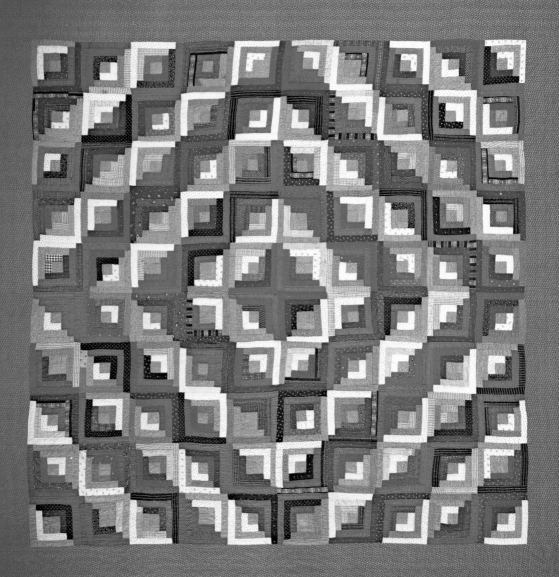

Log Cabin, barn raising,
New Mexico, c. 1900.

New Mexico Barn, 1973.

Rosie and Joe Fischer, Rowlett, Texas, 1974.

aside. He works all day doin' people's yards. Says he don't have to hear out there and everything else he hears makes him nervous. So in the evenin's when he comes in he turns on that little TV and just lays there on the couch watchin' pictures. And I set right here at my quiltin'.

Maybe that don't sound like much, but it's not lonesome. I was real lonesome once after my first husband died and I don't want no more of that.

And he cooks supper ever other night. Gives me more time to be at my work. And I'm grateful for the cookin'.

He ain't lonesome either.

Me and Jack been right here on this place since 1904. He's been here longer. He built everything on this place and plowed every inch of field. There ain't nothin' gone to waste here yet, and there won't ever be. We don't leave nothin' on the plate.

You go around this place, honey, and it most probably just looks like a bunch of junk and scrap to you. Let me show you somethin'. See them old bent rusty nails in that lard can? Makes tomatoes grow the prettiest you ever saw. Them corn cobs in them barrels . . . Cut them in chunks and plow them under and they gonna hold the water around the roots when there ain't no rain.

That bag of calico, denim, and the like. It's kept covers on this growing family since 1904.

We had an ole dog a man give us. He followed us down to the bottoms one night to a fish fry and got girl-friended. Yep, followed her right out into the road and a truck hit him. I tell you a big hunk come in my throat when that dog died. Everthing around here has just about gone now. We ain't got nothin' no more but chickens and dogs and cats. We got our own private buryin' ground out here for our livin' things. We've always buried 'em right.

Tumbling Blocks,
Oklahoma, c. 1875,
Cooper and Buferd Collection.

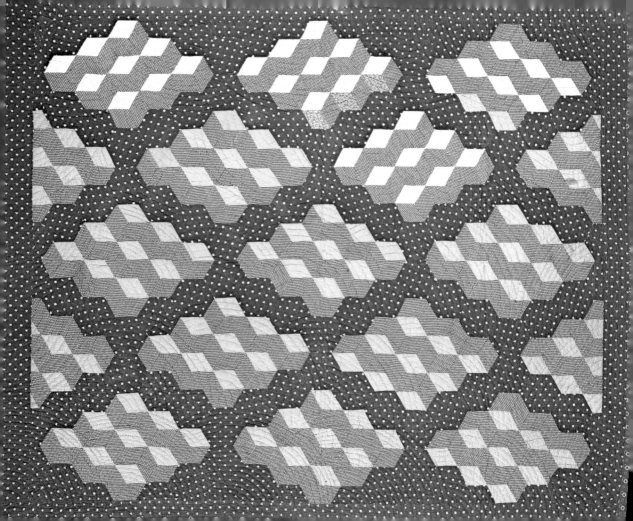

Rosie Fischer, Rowlett, Texas, 1974.

I never quilted for the public. Papa said that wasn't never going to be necessary for us. He's the hardest-workin' man I've ever knowed. He began clearin' the place and farmin' it with nothin' but his own back and a pair of pretty bad old mules. But he done it all and he done it good.

I taken care of the clothes and the cookin' and cannin', the house and the kids. It was always sunup to sundown for us. But the Lord's been good to us. One never worked no less than the other. And I love the ole boy like I did when I was a girl.

I done a quilt on the halves for a friend of mine the other day. The way she pieced it there wasn't no way to quilt it except crooked. I hate to put out work that's crooked. I measure mine and then when I get ready to put it on the frame, if it's true it fits perfect. I make mine thataway.

I never stopped makin' my quilts through all these years. When Papa was out behind them mules, I was keeping my scraps caught up. Now my fingers done got old and the mules are gone.

But I told my ole man that folks is likin' my quilts again and he may find hisself the only farmer that knows how to plow with mules.

Rosie and Joe Fischer, under their wedding picture,
Rowlett, Texas, 1974.

Robbing Peter to Pay Paul, Colorado, c. 1875,
collection of the Pioneer Museum, Colorado Springs, Colorado.

*Mrs. W. M. Garten and Mrs. Vera Leeters
at their quilting bee in Clovis, New Mexico, 1973.*

Well, girls, here they are; just like I said. They come to quilt when the pecans was falling.

Move over there, you old hens. Who's got my thread?

Lord, she done put Dacron inside this outing quilt.

Wear my fingers to the bone looking at it.

I thought I'd never get out here. First he wants me to put my quilting in the outhouse, then he tries to keep me from getting at it.

Had your Shurfine pickles today, Annie?

I gotta leave at noon to take Aunt Lucy her lunch. She's down again.

Go by my kitchen on the way. There's beans on the back burner. Cut your time in half.

This here's the mama of my son's wife. Those two kids made one mess of a house.

When these pieces was put together they kindly made a triple star. When you look at it thisaway you can see a triple star. When you look at it thataway you see boxes.

When I look at it anyway I get dizzy. Mary Lou, you pieced one seasick quilt.

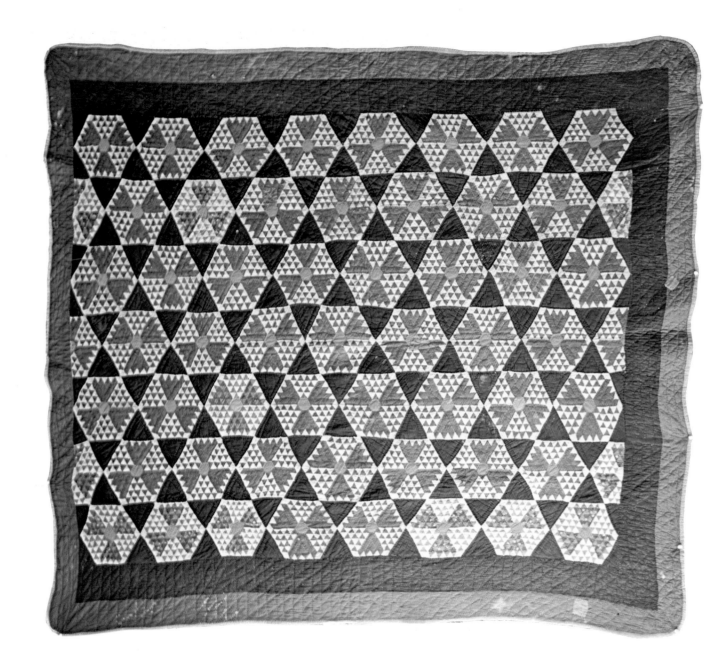

Mrs. A. I. Metcalf,
Clovis, New Mexico, 1974.

Tiny Triangles, c. 1875,
New Mexico.

My boy Jim, and some other of them old men, always find out where we're quilting. And at dinnertime here come their faces. They sit around poking fun, but we pay 'em no mind. Jim's wife still can't understand why he wants to come eat at his momma's with a bunch of old hens. We just grin.

I quilt some everyday. It just keeps me going. When I quilt I just set down here and go at it. I never liked to quilt with a group, only with my mother when I was young. She taught me to quilt and we liked it to always be right. I don't like somebody else working on my quilt. You know, maybe they didn't learn the way I did.

I sit here and quilt facin' this way most of the time. See, I put all my family pictures up there in front of me so I can look at them while I quilt. They are all around me that way.

I have my son up there four times. When he was small and playin', when he graduated from high school, when he was in the war, and with his grandchildren. I look at all those boys and men and think on him.

There's my daughter looking to be the same age as my aunt. They were a lot like one another, too. But, of course, my aunt had passed on before my girl was even born. It's a pleasure puttin' it all together.

There's no way in the world I could even guess how many quilts I've worked in my time. But I do know that I've supplied a lot of households with them. My husband was a minister and we were always involved in charity, either gettin' it or givin' it. So when I was younger I had a stack of quilts that was higher than your head, just inside the front door in the hallway. I used them for gifts—Christmas, weddings, and to divide with the poor. Now all the quilts I have are for my five kids and for all the grandchildren. And now their kids are wanting quilts of their own. I just tell them that as long as they keep bringin' me scraps and likin' my quilts, I'll keep doin'.

I like to do that little half square. A body never throws a bit of scrap in the trash piecin' that one. You can use it all. And they come out real bright and pretty. I get a good feelin' workin' on that one.

Tiny Triangles,
Oklahoma, c. 1900,
Cooper and Buferd Collection.

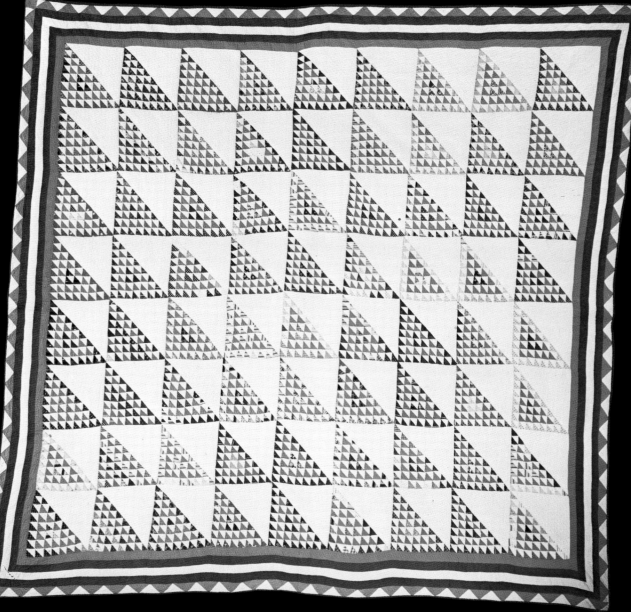

I do my piecing by feel. I can't hardly see nothin' no more. People don't believe I pieced those. I pieced this one after I was nearly blind and you can just turn it over and look at my stitches. They are little, let me tell you. I can thread a needle still. I just point and thread. No, really I have a little invention that I do just like a puzzle. Don't need no help for that. I pieced quilts when I was a child. It's natural for me to sew and make things. My whole family pieced, but I think I cap 'em all. That's not nice for me to say, but I was the oldest girl and learned the longest with Mama.

I want to show you this quilt. And if anybody asks you, I will sell some of these dirt cheap. I have twenty quilts here now, and I have given away about thirty. Now this one here is like a puzzle. See, it has a star and a ninepatch, and I don't know what all. I have a friend in Oklahoma that's a great hand to piece quilts, and she gave me the pattern and I brought it home with me. It's a lot of fun to do. I can't even remember how to do it now. My stepmother pieced this quilt and I think it's real pretty. I cut the colors out for her to piece. I just love to work with quilts. They make a big old mess; you know what I mean? But I just love it. This is a string quilt. You get to use all your little pieces making one of these.

I've made several quilts for people who had the misfortune to burn out and lose all their bedding, and other things. Our club makes quilts for folks in times of trouble. I quilt in a club that sometimes quilts two quilts in one day. We go and have a covered-dish lunch and work all day.

When we was little and moved out to this territory it was plenty cold in the winter, and we had to get busy right away and make quilts for the younger kids. Mama had a few worn-out things and I remember some people gave us some scraps. My grandmother lived with us most of the time and she was a good hand to quilt, and she knitted too. But quilting then was the big object, and we would quilt about eight or ten quilts a year. But you see there was so many of us, it took lots of quilts. My mother had a stack of quilts when she died, and I told my stepmother to save we children one apiece. I have one of them now. I'll get up in the closet and show it to you if you want to see it. It's high, but I don't intend to ever fall. Here's the one my mama made. It's set together in rows like slats in a fence. She called it Fence Row. They used to make lots of quilts like that.

Now my grandmother gave me this and it is older than I am. These tiny blocks all matches except in this one corner. As a little girl, I used to wonder why she didn't get some more of the right color to finish it with. I remember this patch here . . . that was the dress my grandmother had that was so pretty to me then. I can just remember her in that.

Most people don't like to quilt. They think it's too little a business, I guess. Too much work involved. I love to quilt. My husband used to say, "I just have to choke you off a quilt." He did want me to come and eat when the family did, of course. But oh, I'd rather quilt than eat when I'm hungry.

Rocky Road to Kansas . . . I guess they named it that for a purpose. People thought a lot about roads in the old days. Specially when they didn't have any. Seems the road got important enough to name a quilt after anyways. When you was in a wagon train and didn't have no road to follow . . . now that rocky road meant hard times to Kansas. But in them days when you made a road, the thing you remembered most about it was the rocks you had to move. Rocky Road to Oklahoma they sometimes call it too. Makin' new roads through the rocks.

That county road out yonder is jest like a lifeline to me. A body just don't have to work near so hard, nor worry near so much when you know that the road is hard and dry. If you need to get to town, or if the doctor needs to get out here, it can jest be done.

Mrs. Herron quilting
Makin' Tracks to Oklahoma,
Clovis, New Mexico, 1974.

Texas homestead, 1974.

But folks got things done somehow. I remember when the census taker come.

When we first put up the house on the ranch there wasn't no roads nor anything else but mesquite as far as the eye could see. That fall, Bill had gone off to scare up some money working roundup in Concho County. I don't remember just off how many kids I had then but I know Jess and Jim was up big enough to take care of the stock 'cause it was Jess come runnin' to say the cow must have got loose. They couldn't find her nowhere, so there must be a break in the fence. She was my milk cow and I went out after her. I grabbed up my gear to mend the fence.

I left the baby with the littler ones and told 'em to make sure and pick her up ever time she cried and eat some bread till I got back. Bill had took the good horse and the boys had the other one down somewhere with the stock, so I struck out cross country on foot after that cow thinkin' she couldn't have gone too far. Well I kept going and going and after a while my skirt was catching on mesquite and prickly pear. Oh I was a mess, and ever time I wanted to sit down and rest I'd think how I'd gone dry, from overwork I guess, and the baby needed milk and the little kids. Well, I found the hole and mended the fence and by this time it was moving on in the afternoon but I was mad by now and I went after that cow again.

Finally I caught up with her cavortin' around, and I started leadin' her back toward the house one foot in front of the other. By this time I'd tucked up my skirt around my waist. Nobody to see and I just didn't care nohow.

When I come close to the house I could hear the baby cryin'. They had her outside in a little ole wagon riding her round and round the yard, bumpin' and runnin'. Well I grabbed her up and went on in, poor little hot, hungry thing, and give her some sugar water. I couldn't hardly move.

Well, I'm tellin' about roads, you know. So the kids commenced to holler they saw a horse. Now there weren't no roads to the ranch and I went to the door.

Here comes this lady riding sidesaddle in a long skirt from out the brush. She had on gloves. Well, I stood and watched. She come right up in the yard and got off that horse and took this big ole book out of her saddlebag. She looked like she was about to drop. She come up to the door and said,

"Are you Mrs. Baker?"

I said, "Yes."

She said, "I'm the census taker. I like to never found you." Then she commenced to cry. Leanin' against the door cryin'.

I said, "Don't cry, woman."

This quilt is going to be our entry in the fair. We're going to quilt it in diamonds. Now, look here, dearie, you go right straight over, then straight down here, and cross over when you get right here.

Oh good gracious. Is that all you've come for? Just to sit there and quilt? That's all you want to do, girl.

I put on a big pot of fresh coffee for you girls. When I get old enough I'm going to learn to drink coffee.

Yep, I just got back from town in time. Got that window shade up to protect his eyes. If I had two men his age to wait on, I don't know what I'd do. He'll be ninety-two the third of March, and I'll be eighty on the tenth. On the fifteenth we'll be married sixty-two years.

You can really tell this is an old top. You can tell by the print. You can't buy print like this no more. They're gettin' a few old-timey-lookin' prints on

147

the market now, but they have a different texture . . . and they're real hard to quilt. Too much polyester or somethin'.

You sure look fancy today, girl.

Oh, what do you mean? My clothes are ever one ready to go to the scrap bag. I'm going to be able to piece quilts for a year.

First school my baby daughter went to, Jimmy was there. She done something to him and he threw water on her. She went and told the teacher on him and he come home. That old woman gave him a spanking and made him so mad he come home. He said, "Old fool. I'll pull every gray hair she has out." I said, "Jimmy, that ain't gonna do you any good." And he calmed down. Then them kids up and married. I'll bet he won't throw no water on her now. She ain't anywhere big as he is, but then he ain't as loud as she is.

Oh boy, here comes another quilter. Listen, you just move your chair in here right now.

I cain't quilt, girl. I didn't even bring my thimble. I just come to pay my debts.

Good Lord, I gotta have me a bedspread.

Well, why don't you fix that quilt? We'll just put yours in after we get this one out and do it next. It's a Fan. Well, we're not 'posed to. We got two from Oklahoma City and three from Mrs. Clyde and four more waitin' to come.

148   Do you remember the Joneses out at Wheatland? They was akin to the

Clovis Senior Citizens
quilting bee,
New Mexico, 1975.

Double Axe Head, Texas, c. 1965, made by Mrs. Woodburn.

Harrises. His father was a Methodist preacher, you know, went around to all the little churches, and their kids was in school at Grady. Well, I sung "Oh, Promise Me" at the wedding and took 'em a quilt . . . that was their daughter that married last week.

"Well," she said, "do you quilt for the public?" And I said, "I believe I do." "Well," she said, "I guess you don't have much to do." "Well," says I, "I've lived here for sixteen years and only three months out of them sixteen years I haven't had a quilt in the frames." "Oh," she said, "you don't have to hurry, do you?" "Sometimes," I said.

That was the talkinest woman! She was a little short woman. He was a great big man had his eyes operated on. She don't give him time to talk. Move over for Marie. Pull your chair in here, woman. How's your girl?

Poorly, but she'll keep the baby. Lord, it feels good to get to some work quilting. I been piecing at the hospital waiting for news.

Reminds me of the time Jim took ill. I finished piecin' that whole Ocean Wave I give to Mary in his hospital room. Well, the nurse used to come in and say, "Mrs. Roberts, you are going to ruin your eyes." She'd turn up the light and as soon as she was gone I'd turn it down. He never did like bright lights.

When my mother was them last days in the county hospital, she said she was worried she hadn't finished June's quilt. "Well," I said, "don't fret, Mama, I'll do it right now." And I did. Went right over to her house where she had that frame up in the living room and I worked all night and into the next morning. Finished it by noon. I went right back to the hospital to tell Mama and she said she could rest easy now. That was the last good thing I was able to do for her.

Quilting a Flower Garden, New Mexico, 1975.

Lucille, did you get that frame of yours back up in the house?

No. It's still out back. He says it's just interfering with his TV, being in the living room, taking up all the room in there and me quilting instead of watching.

I'm gonna fuss at you about that. Seems you should put it over the bed at least.

I like it out back.

He come in with six bushel of peaches from off Jessie's trees. Said, "Did you ever see the like?"

I said, "Yes, in a bad dream." We turned to and started scalding. We put Auntie and Mam to peeling on the back porch. I said, "I got to go off now." And here I am. I'd rather quilt than can any day. Except I know those peaches will taste good come December. Oh, they do eat those cobblers.

I put a little lemon peel in my peach syrup this year.

Did you ever get that recipe from Bessie for her grandmother's fruit cake? It don't have too much stuff in it; just kinda light with a rum flavor. It keeps a long time in the icebox.

I froze my beans this year. Just snapped 'em, bagged 'em, and put 'em in the freezer. Don't plan to pickle any either.

Don't just sit there. Thread me some needles.

Senior Citizens Building, Clovis, New Mexico, 1973.

Seems I can't get enough of reading, even now. I missed that so much out on the ranch. I was a schoolteacher, you know, before I married Axe-Handle, and once we come to the homestead I never had time for books. Seems like it was just one baby after another, and one worry after another. I had ever one of my twelve kids at home and Bill delivered all but four. We was two days from any help anyways. Finally in 1908 we got some neighbors we could get to in two hours by horseback riding hard. When Bill was gone once loggin' it was midwinter and a howlin' norther, I broke water and was havin' too much pain. Feelin' that baby with my hands I knew for certain it was gonna breach. I put the kids to bed to keep warm and told the older ones to keep that fire goin' no matter what. We had a little room tacked onto the back and I got in there on a pallet under my quilts and Lordy did I pray for Bill to come back. He came blowing in that night. Said he just had a feelin'. I was never so glad to see anyone. He pulled that baby out.

Oh, I don't like to think about my quilts. I lost them all in the fire. After that first winter of homesteading, we started to build the big log cabin. It took three years to put up that big house and I helped every step, pregnant or not. We had the three kids when we moved in. And that's the one that burned, right to the ground one night and all my quilts and books with it. We lost all the kids' things too. My momma's quilts was in there with mine. Well, I didn't have the heart to quilt after that . . . at least no fancy quilts. We was always quilting for cover, making up warm block quilts from old wool and the work clothes. But I just tacked them. They was serviceable all right. Everyone put their hand to piecing in the winter. All my boys pieced right along with the girls. It was work that had to be done.

I seen a lotta life and death. Now I know my time is comin', but I get to choose when it's gonna be. Sometimes I wake in my bed in the mornin' and I say to myself, "How about today? How about if you just don't get up?" And I lie there a while and then reach for my pills and I know it ain't gonna be today. You know, I still got some books left to read.

POSTSCRIPT (1988)

During the time that most of these quilters were living their middle years, Patricia Cooper and I were beginning high school in Clovis, New Mexico. We were the new girls in town and not sure of our welcome there. We became fast friends although many of our interests were different. Pat was studying to be a scientist. I was studying rock and roll and dating. We shared a strong mutual desire, however, to get-out-of-town as soon as possible. After high school we left for different colleges, different states, and quite different lives. Pat moved fast in the academic world and became a professor of marine biology at the University of California at Berkeley. She married and had one daughter. I attended a couple of colleges, flew for the airlines, then adopted two babies and several volunteer agencies.

Even with the differences and distances, we stayed in close contact, sharing, as best friends do, all the watershed moments of our lives and many of the mundane details. It was as if we both gained from two life experiences. Each heard the other's "truth" without judgment, which softened the blows of what sometimes seemed to be flubs, failures, or setbacks in our lives.

We were in our thirties when we came together for research on this book. We began it back in the towns that in our younger years we had been so anxious to escape. We were back home finally asking the women there who they were. What were their truths? Would they let us learn from their experiences?

I don't believe the time could have come any sooner for these meetings. Retrospection and reflection were necessary for them and for us. They were ready now to talk about their personal lives and feelings and their art. Their quilts were journals in cloth on which they could focus their remembrances. Their talk was a gift—a gift that became this small book. It was first published in 1977. I think the angels must have approved, because wonderful and amazing things began to happen right away.

The book received the American Library Association's Notable Book Award and the League of Nations Books-Across-the-Seas Award. Other awards followed. Thousands of women of all ages and economic strata began to use quilting as their creative outlet. The original quilting foundations laid by the "scrap piecers of necessity" expanded once again. The textile art of quilting had taken its place. A young midwest farmwife, Chris Edmonds, stitched her farmhouse and every living thing around it into her very first quilt. A California acupuncturist created a quilt depicting all the yin/yang energy points on a scale-size cotton human body. Entire fairy tales on cloth appeared.

I certainly don't assume or imply that these strides happened because of our book, but only that the new interest in quilting kept it in print for twelve years, when the average shelf life for a book is six weeks.

Then friends began to call and tell us that *The Quilters* was being used as a supplementary text in first this university and then that—Harvard, Texas Tech, U.C. Berkeley....The words of *The Quilters*, their strong kind wisdom were being taught in women's studies, sociology, and folklore courses. Pat's daughter, Willa, called home from Vassar when she was given the assignment to read it.

Meanwhile we traveled and lectured, all the while staying in touch with most of the women, who had become like extended family to us. They were receiving fan letters and quilt orders from all over the world. The quilts they had years before folded and stacked like forgotten paintings were now unfurled and hanging in major museum shows with tens of thousands of people admiring them.

Then, when it seemed the rewards of the work couldn't get better, they did. Molly Newman and Barbara Damashek wrote a musical based on the book, calling it *Quilters*. The Denver Center Theatre first produced it. It traveled to most of the major regional theaters in this country and won competitions in Europe. Then Denver was joined by coproducers: the John F. Kennedy Center for the Performing Arts, the American National Theatre and Academy, and Brockman Sewell. They took it to Broadway, where it was nominated for seven Tony Awards.

Now regional theaters, community theaters, universities, and high schools are speaking the words of our quilters and others to large audiences everywhere. Eastern New Mexico University will present it next. Many of the women in that area who spoke with us are no longer living, but Quirl Thompson Havenhill, who is now ninety-one years old, plans to be in the front row.

Patricia Cooper, coauthor, friend, and cherished witness to my life and to the lives of *The Quilters,* died suddenly in 1987. There is sweet consolation. Each time *Quilters* is performed anywhere in the world, at the final curtain a beautiful huge Tree of Life quilt is gently and slowly elevated into the focus of a brilliant white light. A clear, strong feminine voice speaks from the darkness, saying, "Give her of the fruit of her hands; and let her own works praise her in the gates."

Norma Bradley Allen